DATE DUE

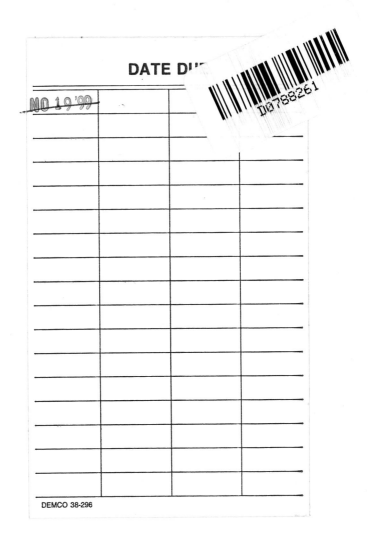

DEMCO 38-296

POWER AND STYLE

POWER AND STYLE

A Critique of
Twentieth-Century Architecture
in the United States

ROBERT
TWOMBLY

HILL AND WANG • *A division of Farrar, Straus and Giroux / New York*

LIBRARY OF CONGRESS CATALOGING-IN-PUBLICATION DATA
Twombly, Robert C.
Power and style : a critique of twentieth-century architecture in
the United States / Robert Twombly.—1st ed.
p.   cm.
Includes bibliographical references and index.
1. Architecture, Modern—20th century—United States.
2. Architecture—United States.   I. Title.
NA712.T88   1996   720′.973′0904—dc20   95–34123   CIP

The text of *Power and Style* originally appeared in *Encylopedia of the United States in the Twentieth Century*, copyright © 1996 by Charles Scribner's Sons.

The present text of *Power and Style* is an expanded and altered version of the text in the *Encylopedia*. In addition, the Hill and Wang edition includes seventy photographs to illustrate the text.

CONTENTS

ILLUSTRATIONS

PREFACE AND
ACKNOWLEDGMENTS

One of the two most respected architects in The Netherlands is Herman Hertzberger (the other is Aldo Van Eyck, and most of what follows could also be said about him), who has devoted his distinguished career to designing social housing, dwellings for the elderly, schools, cultural facilities, town reconstruction plans, and office space. In order to contain costs he specializes in brick and concrete block, which, in his hands, transmit beauty. His principal objective is to create interior spaces flexible enough to accommodate a multiplicity of human activities simultaneously, adaptable enough to cope with change over time. His book, *Lessons for Students in Architecture* (1991), candidly discusses his successes and his failures for the benefit of the next generation. Hertzberger has never designed a private residence.

One of the two most famous architects in the United States is Philip Johnson (the other is I. M. Pei, and most of what follows could also be said about him), who has devoted his long career to designing upper-income housing, art museums, but especially high-rise office structures. With little worry about containing costs, he specializes in luxury materials, which, in his hands, perform the same historic services they have always performed. His principal objective is to create memorable façades and elegant interiors for institutional and corporate clients. His books, *The International Style* (1932) and *Mies van der Rohe* (1947), admiringly applaud the luminaries of his profession for the cognoscenti of the present. Johnson has never designed public housing.

The differences between these architects are less personal, less matters of character or of cultural milieu, than they are consequences of the social relations of design within their respective countries. In The Netherlands since the turn of the twentieth century, the most prominent architects have been hired by the public sector and by workers' organizations to improve the quality of life for the social collectivity. In the United States since the turn of the twentieth century, the most prominent architects have been hired by the elite of the private sector and occasionally by the state to polish their public images or to ennoble their immediate surroundings. In The Netherlands, almost all premier architects since 1900 have designed social housing, which, in numerous cases, constitutes the bulk of their work. In the United States, only a handful of premier architects since 1900 have designed public housing, which has never been the bulk of any such person's work. The ramifications for the United States of these differences is the subject of this book.

Jeanne Chase Twombly helped me wrestle with and understand these ramifications. Her critiques of the manuscript during its various stages of development, as well as our many conversations about the social relations of architecture, have informed my thinking immeasurably. For that, and more, I thank her. Whatever flaws are in this book are not of her making.

I am also grateful for thoughtful readings to Stanley I. Kutler, who commissioned the essay of which this work is an expansion, and to Narciso G. Menocal, who pored over it when he could have been enjoying the pleasures of New York City. Alan Feigenberg clarified a number of legal and organizational niceties of the architectural profession. Arthur Wang at Hill & Wang and Lizabeth Cohen each provided helpful suggestions. Thanks as well to Robert Rosenbaum for his perceptive copyediting.

Special thanks to Mary Woolever of The Art Institute, Chicago, for her patience, generosity, and skill answering innumerable questions while procuring a number of illustrations. She made my task much easier. Others who helped in this regard are cited individually in picture captions but thanked collectively here.

In some ways this book evolved from lectures and discussions about "A Social History of American Architecture," a course I have offered at the City College of New York since 1976. I thank the many fine students there whose observations and ideas continue to stimulate me. At a moment when the City College in particular

and public education in general are increasingly under attack politically, as well as pedagogically, I emphasize here that my contact
with public university students has been consistently more intel-
lectually rewarding than my contact with those from private universities, even those known to be "prestigious."

So it is to past and future City College students that I dedicate
this book.

December 1994

POWER AND STYLE

ARCHITECTS AND SOCIAL PLACE

AT THE CLOSE of the twentieth century, in the United States as elsewhere, there are three kinds of buildings: signature, generic, and vernacular. A handful are designed by highly visible architects known even to the general public as an elite coterie working internationally on glamorous "signature" edifices for public and private organizations with immense financial resources: I. M. Pei with his National Gallery East Wing in Washington, D.C., and his Pyramid at the Louvre in Paris, for example, or Richard Meier with his J. Paul Getty Center in Santa Monica, California, and his Museum für Kunsthandwerk in Frankfurt am Main. A considerably larger second group of buildings is designed by "invisible" architects, unknown except in their immediate vicinities, who put up some of the middle-class and what little there is of public housing in the United States as well as local facilities for governments, public agencies, and business, that is, endless variations on what might be called basic "generic" types. The vast majority of construction—by convention called "vernacular," and it is 95 percent of the nation's total—is not designed by architects at all, but consists of easily replicable structures that developers and contractors assemble for shopping malls, tract housing, and roadside services, for storage and distribution, for franchise, chain, and discount merchandising, and as the rest of that sea of aesthetic minimalism that architect Robert Venturi praised in *Learning from Las Vegas* (1972) but that critic Peter Blake had already decried as *God's Own Junkyard* (1964).

At the beginning of the twentieth century the situation was somewhat different. There were, to be sure, both an elite coterie of architects in the United States, just emerging as a self-conscious group, quite small and without international reputation (except for Henry Hobson Richardson and Richard Morris Hunt, both dead, Louis Sullivan, the firm of McKim, Mead & White, and perhaps a few others) and a largely invisible majority, many of whom are forgotten a hundred years later. The major difference lies in the vernacular, which, in 1900—despite the appearance of building and loan associations and promotional literature like builders' guides and "home-owners" magazines—still by and large meant the traditional forms and construction methods of the amateur or single-occasion builder capable of erecting a dwelling or a shop with or without assistance.

But during the course of the century vernacular came singularly to mean mass-produced construction based on packaged formulas. The Southern rural "dogtrot" house, the Western "false-front," and the Northeastern "saltbox" gradually gave way to the omnipresent "bungalow," the "ranch" and its split-level version, the "splanch," to the shopping strip's Pizza Hut, Midas Muffler, and Dairy Queen outlets, and to countless other easily duplicated ubiquitous building types. Neither earlier nor later vernacular was architect-generated, although on occasion the latter was remotely based on professional designs. The difference is that, whereas every dogtrot house was an idiosyncratic version of a collective building type that had evolved over generations in response to local climates and materials, Dairy Queen and the ranch house conflated time and place. If suburban shelter on Long Island or even the Great Plains bears little resemblance today to what cattle-raising families required a hundred years ago, neither does the Pizza Hut roof, call it mansard or shed, reveal much about the seventeenth-century design intentions of François Mansart or about agricultural storage spaces. What modern vernacular does reveal, however, is disregard for regional and temporal difference.

In addition to dissociation from historical time and specific place, modern vernacular also embodies a trickle-down process, a kind of architectural Reaganomics, only more effective, wherein ideas originating with the visible elite are homogenized by invisible colleagues in their own designs or by contractors and developers (who are required by most municipalities to pay a licensed architect or engineer to approve plans ex post facto). Take as an example the free-standing pediment pierced by a hole of 1980s "postmodernism." It is difficult to determine who introduced this element, but

1. Stanley Tigerman, "Daisy House" (1975–78), Porter, Indiana. *Photo by Howard N. Kaplan © HNK Architectural Photography. Courtesy Tigerman McCurry Architects*

2. Saturn of West Nyack (New York) automobile agency (early 1990s). *Photo by Robert Twombly*

it was surely a well-known architect, possibly Stanley Tigerman in the form of an entry arch at his 1975–78 "Daisy House" (fig. 1) in Porter, Indiana. Whatever the source, by the 1990s the holey pediment was found at suburban shopping malls, atop skyscrapers, as new crowns for rehabilitated nineteenth-century business blocks, and on automobile showrooms (fig. 2), indeed, on every imaginable kind of structure. Originating as an ornamental fillip for clients of means, it became a device for upgrading downscale buildings before devolving into a cliché for mass consumption.

The transformation of vernacular from folk to standardized forms mirrored the rise of a hegemonic architectural elite—the former was a consequence of the latter—both processes having been completed around midcentury. Although little-known architects and commercial builders are still responsible for more than nine-tenths of the nation's constructed fabric, visible architects control the profession. Only they can advertise themselves by collaborating with "critics" on coffee-table monographs about their own work. Only they are featured on national television, taken up by national magazines (including Sunday supplements), or asked to design shopping bags for Bloomingdale's. By shaping the content of the American Institute of Architects (AIA) guidelines, the visible elite affects local and state affiliates that, among other things, influence fee structures, licensing and accreditation criteria, and determine their own memberships. Visible architects launch trendy stylistic mannerisms, set the agenda for polemical debate, influence the content of national and regional design journals, and often double as directors of prestigious training schools. Without elite sponsorship—without attending one of a handful of premier schools and later working for a prominent firm—it is nearly impossible to rise above the ranks of the invisible. The graduate of a publicly funded school of architecture like the City College of New York or the University of Wisconsin–Milwaukee, for example, may have spent more time studying statics, structures, and mechanical systems (that is, what makes a building work) and less time studying history, theory, and critical opinion (that is, what makes a building famous) than an Ivy League counterpart, but will find it infinitely more difficult to hire on with a "star" architect and thus eventually open a visible "shop."

Rigid stratification is the consequence of a professionalizing process that by 1900 was well under way and accelerating. Its beginnings may conveniently be dated with the formation of AIA in 1857 and was essentially completed by World War II. As professionalization gathered momentum during the 1890s, it generated two desiderata not new to architects but for the first time pursued collectively and consciously, as opposed to individually and unconsciously. One was the necessity, in public perception and in fact, to sever ties with what were now deemed the lesser endeavors of construction and engineering, this because an emerging elite within what had historically been a masterly craft chose to define itself as a select group of artists, as creative persons, whose calling was nobler and of greater consequence than that of mere artisan-builders. The second desideratum involved social location: the desire of leading architects to elevate themselves from a comparatively powerless, loosely associated group of independent gentlemen into a tightly knit appendage of the ruling class.

The two desiderata intersected because only as artists—certainly not as craftsmen—would architects be indispensable to a new, still-emerging business elite aware of its own shaky social credentials—its lack of historical rootedness and cultural connoisseurship—by providing it with visual emblems of social standing. Legitimizing economic power with artistic excellence addressed the objectives of both purchaser and provider, but it was not solely through service to well-placed individuals that architects found opportunity to advance their own agenda. For during the late nineteenth century the demands of a new network of architectural patrons—corporations and the republican state as well as plutocrats—surpassed in volume those of an older network—church, monarchy, and aristocracy—to which U.S. architects for obvious reasons had never had much access. The new demands were symbolic as well as material, political as well as social, and equally if not more oriented than those of the older network toward individual and institutional self-valorization.

Just as the social objectives of individuals and their organizations overlapped those of architects, so did the political objectives of the republican state. Its internal enemies in the decades bracketing the turn of the century, principally organizing labor and radical political movements, were also architects' enemies for quite tangible reasons: all visible U.S. architects opposed unionization, especially in the building trades, where struggles for and implementation of higher wages, safety measures, injury compensation, and the eight-hour day slowed construction while raising its costs. No U.S. architect of note, including stylistic "progressives" like Louis Sullivan and Frank Lloyd Wright, was associated with the political left as were prominent Europeans like H. P. Berlage in The Netherlands, Tony Garnier in France, and Ernst May in Germany. The republican state's external objectives, furthermore, the expansion of economic and territorial empire overseas, helped solidify a national self-image of cultural exclusivity and superiority to which architects adhered and were also internalizing personally and as a group. By cloaking public and private entities in artistic imagery intended to validate the social order, architects not only embraced that order but also found a way to assume a more privileged position within it. The images were carefully chosen to suggest analogies—that is, to obscure the very real differences—between American social and political intentions and European social and political achievement, and were mostly culled from history. Because scholars have grouped those images under the socially neutral rubric of "eclecticism," it is easy to overlook the precision with which they were applied.

There were dissenters from this historicizing impulse—this eclectic use of the past—to be sure. Principally in the Midwest, a younger generation inspired by Henry Hobson Richardson and Louis Sullivan argued that to develop contemporary expressions of time and place was more important than to perpetuate ancient forms or adapt foreign ideas. Their position was encapsulated in the slogan "Progress before Precedent," adopted in 1900 by the year-old Architectural League of America, in its first half decade a rebellious organization whose members had mostly started working in the 1880s and 1890s. Their argument was not with the notion of national superiority or exceptionalism, however, and rarely with the practices of plutocracy and state; nor was it with the social ambitions of architects or the political meaning of design. Rather, the League concentrated on aesthetics, maintaining that eclecticism should be replaced by an "American" style or, put another way, that historical architecture had outlived its usefulness. Many former members of the Western Association of Architects, another somewhat rebellious group before it merged with AIA in 1889, agreed with the League only to find themselves opposed by the conservative larger body. By confining the discussion almost exclusively to matters of style, however, turn-of-the-century practitioners—whether "traditionalists" basing designs on historical "precedent" or "rebels" advocating "progress"—removed their work from any other than formal analysis, where it has by and large remained except for a minority of observers. Unlike most other architectures, that of the United States has been praised and condemned, debated, discussed, and criticized, more often in terms of aesthetics than in terms of social relations.

STYLE AND SOCIAL AGENDA, 1890–1910

EVEN SO, it is exceedingly difficult to maintain, as many have, that a national style has ever existed. There have certainly been building types—the skyscraper springs first to mind—and ways of expressing them—Louis Sullivan's, of course—that were invented here. Frank Lloyd Wright and his "prairie school" followers developed a residential model that specifically rejected other times and places. Ludwig Mies van der Rohe realized with steel, concrete, and glass what neither he nor others had in other countries. But in the long view of history these modes of articulation were only briefly à la mode, no matter their profound influence; nor do three discrete mannerisms, or even ten or twenty, add up to a national style. U.S. architects, in other words, have not developed anything like a Gothic or a Baroque to which it might be said there was culturewide or even elite commitment over a long duration. Such commitment is more likely found in the realms of folk and even commercial building, but not in the fine art of design.

There were periods before the mid-nineteenth century, to be sure, when particular conventions and mannerisms dominated regions or captured national fancy. Adaptations of Dutch, English, French, and Spanish forms prevailed in appropriate areas of colonial settlement. Some historians claim the so-called Federalist style as the first national architecture, but during its heyday at the turn of the nineteenth century it was in fact a late and localized (heavily in the Northeast) version of English Georgian that had gingerly entered the colonies early in the eighteenth century to achieve wide acceptance around 1760. Geographically broader in appeal was the Greek Revival of the 1820s to 1840s (lingering longer in the Old Northwest), also claimed by some as the first national style, mostly on the basis of ubiquity—begging the question, as is also the case with the Federalist style, of whether an adaptation of an overseas mannerism can be considered indigenous—followed by the chronologically overlapping Gothic Revival, which lost its momentum with the outbreak of civil war.

From roughly the 1860s until World War I the nation's architecture was no longer characterized by a succession of adaptations (Federalist, Greek, and Gothic) or by regional mannerisms co-existing in time but not necessarily in space (as in the colonial period). The last four decades of the nineteenth century were, rather, an era of extraordinary diversity on a continental scale; historic and recent styles from over the world flooded the nation but no one prevailed even locally or regionally. All was not as chaotic as it might seem, however; there were certain selecting and organizing principles in the eclectic potpourri. One was the use of specific styles for particular building types: Gothic for universities and churches, including Protestant churches; neoclassical and neo-Renaissance (sometimes called "Beaux Arts" after the École des Beaux-Arts in Paris) for financial institutions and government structures; "round-arch," a kind of simplified Romanesque for commerce and warehousing; Tudor, "Italianate," "Queen Anne," and many others for suburban and country villas.

A second organizing principle addressed a middle-class desire: to differentiate one's own dwelling from what were fundamentally similar houses next door and across the street; for structures that were essentially the same size and shape, set back the same distance from the sidewalk and from each other, and with the same room designations, clients could insist upon a classical pediment here or a Tudor window there to reclaim their individuality. Or eclecticism could be organized in more idiosyncratic ways by administering myriad historical flourishes to a single building, Frank Furness's Pennsylvania Academy of the Fine Arts (1871–76) in Philadelphia, for example, sporting touches of neo-Gothic, neo-Greek, French Second Empire, Egyptian Revival, Romanesque, and neoclassical salted with elements from an artful cornucopia of his own concoction (fig. 3). Furness's was truly an "international" style that, under the name "High Victorian Gothic" and side by side with other eclecticisms, made the typical late-nineteenth-century U.S. street an architectural league of nations. Despite increasing clamor for culturally indigenous expressions, the na-

3. Frank Furness, Pennsylvania Academy of the Fine Arts (1871–76), Philadelphia. *Courtesy The Art Institute, Chicago*

tion's architect-designed buildings were adaptations—but almost never direct imitations—of usually historic, sometimes contemporary, but virtually always non-American structures.

Rummaging the world for historical inspiration may have been especially pronounced in English-speaking countries, the United States perhaps most of all, possibly because it lacked long-standing, universally agreed-upon traditions of its own. But another factor was the extraordinary influence here of the English critic John Ruskin and the French architect Eugène-Emmanuel Viollet-le-Duc, which might in part be explained by the United States not yet having comparably authoritative homegrown art theorists. Ruskin's insistence that proper architecture was a moral force for social improvement and Viollet-le-Duc's emphasis on structural rationalism struck chords of recognition that resonated in other areas of American culture, but their wide acceptance was also based on a shared preference for the Gothic, albeit gothics of very different sorts. The genius of visible eclectic architects in the United States, however, was to stand Ruskin on his head and to trivialize the import of Viollet-le-Duc.

Ruskin's interests were with working people, but visible eclectics' were with employers. For him, good architecture would uplift the masses; for them, good architecture would keep the masses in their place while uplifting their patrons. All agreed that architecture could be a moral force. The question was: to whose benefit? Viollet-le-Duc argued that good architecture clearly and rationally revealed its structural systems, best demonstrated by French Gothic. U.S. architects, ignoring the essential message that structure should determine form, took away only the notion that Gothic was rational and could thus serve as the compositional basis of a skyscraper, for example, to signal the efficient, rationalized business activities housed inside. Both theorists were thus divested of progressive implication—in the one case social, in the other aesthetic—and made to serve the prevailing social and aesthetic order.

In the hands of an eclectic elite, modern functions and building systems were ordinarily disguised with socially loaded ornamentation, composition, and form. It remained for stylistic progressives to embrace structural rationalism, perhaps in part to muster authority for their artistic waywardness, which afforded them little access to elite and state patronage. During the middle third of the twentieth century, ironically enough, structural rationalism would be taken up by second- and third-generation descendants of the late-nineteenth-century elite, administering a temporary setback to latter-day eclectics. But around the turn of the century specific classical, medieval, and Renaissance models were selected as vehicles for appropriating Ruskin's sense of social purpose to the exclusive benefit of the powerful and well placed. The following examination of plutocratic residences, government edifices, and quasi-public structures will demonstrate that eclecticism was never socially neutral nor randomly applied.

The very rich were drawn to several styles for the dwellings with which they declared their social arrival, but what architectural historian Marcus Whiffen calls the "châteauesque," typified by Richard Morris Hunt's work for the Vanderbilt family, and the neo-Renaissance, popularized in the United States by McKim,

Mead & White, were the most exclusive. What the two shared and perhaps exhibited better than other possibilities was their association with prior aristocracies.

The châteauesque is sometimes called the Francis I style and in its sixteenth-century inception was a synthesis of Italian Renaissance and native Gothic forms. During the second quarter of the nineteenth century it underwent a revival in France at just the moment that Hunt—the first American to do so—was studying at the École des Beaux-Arts. The first major realization of the style in this country was his 1882 mansion (fig. 4) on Fifth Avenue, New York, for William K. Vanderbilt, a building understood by the leading American architecture critic, Montgomery Schuyler, to refer "to the romantic classicism of the great châteaux of the Loire." The many other designers Hunt influenced promptly followed the Vanderbilt precedent with lesser counterparts, but the most lavish ever constructed in the United States was Hunt's own "Biltmore" (1888–95) for George Washington Vanderbilt near Asheville, North Carolina, over a thousand feet long (with stables) at the center of 120,000 acres laid out by Frederick Law Olmsted. Soon the Michigan, Woodward, and Commonwealth avenues of the nation's cities and the Newport and North Shore vacation colonies were dotted with Loire and other châteaux, collectively the most lavish architectural manifestation of recently acquired personal wealth ever seen in this country.

Also important was the neo-Renaissance, introduced here by McKim, Mead & White for Henry Villard's 1882–85 house group (fig. 5) on New York's Madison Avenue. Neither Charles F. McKim nor Stanford White had studied abroad. Both had attended the newly established architecture department (the nation's first) at the Massachusetts Institute of Technology and apprenticed with Henry Hobson Richardson before teaming up with William Rutherford Mead. It is instructive to compare the social location of their clients with his.

Richardson, who was uncomfortable with neoclassical forms, sometimes worked with aggressive entrepreneurs like Marshall Field and John Jacob Glessner in Chicago, the Cheney department store family in Hartford, and the Ames industrialists in Massachusetts. But those with whom he preferred to associate, including a number of his clients, represented an older, socially established, often Harvard-educated, Yankee elite involved with regional com-

4. Richard Morris Hunt, William K. Vanderbilt residence (1882), New York. *From Susan R. Stein, ed.,* The Architecture of Richard Morris Hunt

merce and manufacturing, public service, and the arts: men like John Hay, Henry Adams, Phillips Brooks, Frederick Law Olmsted, and Francis Lee Higginson. McKim, Mead, and White, on the other hand, who opened their office in 1879, fourteen years after Richardson had opened his, attached themselves to a newer, much wealthier, more powerful, but socially less established oligarchy

5. McKim, Mead & White, Henry Villard residences (1882–85), New York. *From Alfred Hoyt Granger*, Charles Follen McKim: A Study of His Life and Work

6. Henry Hobson Richardson, John J. Glessner residence (1885–87), Chicago.

comprising nationally oriented industrial and financial barons: rail-road promoter Henry Villard, traction magnate William C. Whit-ney, Oliver Payne of Standard Oil, Jay Gould's broker Charles Osborn, members of J. P. Morgan's family, Cyrus McCormick, and the like. To accommodate *his* clients, Richardson experi-mented at first with historic styles, finally settling on variations of the Romanesque (fig. 6), which he developed so far beyond the original inspiration as to earn the label "Richardsonian Roman-esque," indicating that he had invented his own architectural lan-guage. To accommodate *their* clients, McKim, Mead & White went in another direction, passing through Richardson's and other man-nerisms to settle on the Renaissance palazzo, particularly the pa-lazzi of Florence. The choice made perfect sense.

The fifteenth-century "boom in the construction of family *pa-lazzi*," Lauro Martines writes, was the result of "a growing con-centration of wealth." Some hundred new palaces plus the expansion of many older villas were erected in Florence alone in the 1400s. This building and rebuilding "craze," he adds, was "the very process of élite consciousness," "a growing resolution to re-make or reshape the things around. . . . In effect, this was the quest for greater control over immediate environments." Princes, oligarchs, and other rich men "sought to affirm themselves by means of imposing *palazzi*, more organized and splendid façades," more elaborate interiors, decorations, and objects. The "passion" with which they "displayed their high status or proved their virtue," Martines continues, extended beyond *palazzi* to other "architec-tural projects such as churches, chapels, . . . and new public buildings." "As the political and monied élites spread out and pre-empted more urban space, all others had to be content with less." Ultimately, "the rising awareness that élites could reapportion or remake the urban space if they so willed" led to an interest in ideal cities, which was "politically a deeply conservative concep-tion, a response," he concludes, "to the rising demand by princes and urban élites for grandeur and show, order and ample space, finesse and finished surfaces."

And so too in the late-nineteenth-century United States. New, industrially based owners, still first or second generation in the 1890s and harboring a nagging sense of social insecurity, wanted to make their cultural mark, to distinguish themselves from the rest of society, to express their impressive power, perhaps also to disguise from themselves and others the grubby ways in which they had accumulated that power. "There is nothing about a château after the manner of Blois," Jeanne Chase has written, "to remind its occupant about the railroad on which that château is based."

So it is not surprising that the American counterpart to the Quattrocento oligarchy should have forsworn the circumspect brick and brown stone townhouses of eighteenth- and early-nineteenth-century elites for granite châteaux and marble palazzi. Or, like their Florentine predecessors, should have sponsored privately funded civic projects like libraries, museums, opera houses, universities, even municipal plans all, almost invariably, in the neoclassical mannerisms based upon Renaissance forms. The Quattrocento was far enough removed in time for its seamier means of wealth and power accumulation to be conveniently forgotten in the American process of identification with it, but it remained so architecturally potent, if not hallowed, as to be reified into an endorsement of the new social order, of the legitimacy of the new national elite.

No matter the style—Florentine, Loire Valley, or something else—it was European aristocracies to which U.S. architects referred when they designed mansions for the rich. And if that historicism was intended to validate those rich and, in addition, to persuade an older elite to accept new members, it nevertheless filtered down through the social hierarchy to middle-class dwellings in wood rather than stone, with eight rooms rather than fifty, on Roxbury side streets near trolley lines rather than Drexler Boulevard with carriage lanes, and from there further down to decorative touches over doors and windows and along the cornices of working-class tenements in South Philadelphia and New York's Lower East Side. No matter that working families were packed into these buildings like sardines. Aristocracy-referring architecture proclaimed every man a king, someday anyway.

Such was the message directed toward working-class immigrants even before they reached those tenements, as they arrived at the Ellis Island reception center in New York harbor. Federal takeover of immigrant processing in 1891, together with the destruction by fire of the island's original facilities six years later, required a new building, designed in 1898 by the New York firm of Boring & Tilton. In his review that year of plans for "such quarters . . . as were never seen before on this side of the Atlantic," a *New York*

Times reporter concluded that so grand was the architecture that even the poorest newcomer could "indulge in the inexpensive pleasure of imagining that in his role [as] a future American monarch the Republic has placed at his disposal a palace far . . . handsomer than many of those . . . in the Old World."

Opened in 1900, Boring & Tilton's building held out hope of upward mobility but also laid down rules on how to achieve it. In what was then called "French Renaissance" but is now referred to as "Beaux Arts classical" style, the processing center exemplified the notion that Greek and Roman structural systems could be codified and synthesized. The style and its archaeological impulse reached their zenith in the United States in the 1890s and 1900s, mostly with prominent public and quasi-public edifices like Hunt's 1892 Administration Building at the Chicago World's Fair, his 1895 Metropolitan Museum of Art in New York, and Carrère and Hastings's New York Public Library (1895–1902). Used to commemorate patriotic heroism as with Palmer and Hornbostel's Allegheny County Soldiers and Sailors Memorial (1905–8) in Pittsburgh or for imposing urban portals like Warren and Wetmore's Grand Central Terminal (1903–10) in New York, Beaux Arts classicism made its greatest impact at early-twentieth-century international expositions, Bernard Maybeck's 1915 Palace of the Fine Arts at San Francisco's Panama–Pacific Exposition being perhaps its finest expression. The purpose of this architectural style was to impress the public with majesty and grandeur.

Like monumental railroad terminals of the period, Ellis Island's reception center was also a portal—hinting at wonders beyond its doors—not for a city but for an entire nation, and as such directed attention toward the government whose edifice it was. This was done architecturally (fig. 7) by the striking contrast in color and texture between its imposing redbrick walls and its ebullient gray stone trim, and by the overscaled heraldry and pilasters separating three larger-than-necessary arches at the entry. It was done by the prominence of four corner towers—capped with brilliant copper domes—that thickened as they descended, and by the assertive entablature partially blocking and thus accentuating semicircular attic windows. And it was done with crisp, copper-faced gables playing against the sloping clerestory roof. This was an architecture of contrast and exaggeration, designed to make a strong impact on arrivals even before they docked.

Other design elements were intended to transform entry

through the massive central pavilion into a memorable event, which was extended through time and space up the grand staircase to the Registry Room (fig. 8), 200 feet long by 100 wide, under a 56-foot vaulted ceiling. Three elaborate electroliers supplemented eight arched windows rising from an inspection gallery ringing the room. The scale, noise, and brightness surely produced the desired effect upon those who had never seen artificial light or witnessed such a vast and busy interior except, perhaps, in church. A building "of so much architectural pretension," an observer noted, could hardly fail to attract the "attention . . . and the bovine stare of the dazed immigrant" who was being told in an intimidating situation that would continue beyond the portal that it was no doubt wise to heed the wisdom and respect the power that had created such a magnificent architectural display.

Government architecture in general—state, local, and federal —embodied similar ideas, less often in Beaux Arts style than in a more highly refined neoclassicism referring directly to ancient Greece and Rome without fifteenth-century mediation. By and large neoclassical buildings were bigger, simpler, and of cleaner line than those in the Beaux Arts manner. They tended to monochromes of gray or white, with less assertive sculptural and decorative flourishes, fewer projections and recesses along their façades, and less elaborate attics. Given considerable momentum by the 1893 World's Columbian Exposition in Chicago—which received over 21 million visitors, equivalent to one-third the national population—and by the civic-center component of the "City Beautiful" planning movement it spawned, neoclassicism dominated government architecture into the 1930s.

As the United States assumed "the white man's burden" overseas and encountered increasingly determined opposition to its collaboration with organized wealth at home, Greek- and Roman-inspired police headquarters, city halls, courthouses, and state capitols mushroomed around the nation, followed after World War I by war memorials in Europe and embassies elsewhere. Chicago's prominent neoclassicist, Daniel H. Burnham, who was also the premier city planner in the United States, spoke for the elite of his profession in 1906 when he declared that the ceremonial sector of his Manila scheme would "put to the test . . . notable examples from the days of old Rome." Well known among the many domestic expressions of ancient architecture are George B. Post's 1904 Wis-

7. Boring & Tilton, Main Building (1898–1900), Ellis Island, New York Harbor. *Courtesy Beyer Blinder Belle/ Notter Finegold & Alexander Architects, Inc.*

8. Boring & Tilton, Registry Room (1898–1900), Main Building, Ellis Island, New York Harbor. *Courtesy New York Public Library*

consin State Capitol (fig. 9) in Madison, the Shelby County Court-house (1907) by Hale and Rogers in Memphis, and, of course, most of Washington, D.C. Elsewhere are Egerton Swartwout's St. Mihiel Monument (*c.* 1923) in Montsec, France, J. E. Campbell's embassy (1925) in Mexico City, and Jay Morgan's consulate (1932) in Yokohama.

Greek and Roman architectures were immensely serviceable to U.S. governments for ideological reasons. Other Western nations were drawn to neoclassicism around the turn of the century but, according to an authority on the history of this nation's styles, the "revival in its entirety [had] no parallel on the other side of the Atlantic. . . . Nowhere outside the United States were the classical orders . . . drawn up in so many parade formations." The sheer quantity of production here was staggering. "More marble was used in building in the United States in the years 1900–1917," writes Marcus Whiffen, "than . . . in the Roman Empire during its entire history." But even more significant was the intensity of commitment to what Greek and Roman architectures were said to represent as well as to what they in fact represented in, perhaps, a more subliminal way.

By 1900 the United States had successfully constructed one kind of empire—territorial across the continent—and was building another—economic as well as territorial—overseas. In service to economic expansion or not, federal officials spoke endlessly about the national mission to spread democratic ideals, which Greek architecture was said to represent. At the same time, indigenous peoples overseas and in the American West, not to mention native- and foreign-born farm and factory laborers all around the country, were refusing in various ways to live happily with new police- and military-backed impositions of power aiming to order their lives. Populism, socialism, the International Workers of the World, and other radical movements were at their strongest between 1900 and 1917, and shattering disruptions like the 1886 Haymarket massacre and the 1894 Pullman strike—only tips of the iceberg of social unrest—remained vivid for everyone.

To republican governments, the social order was under attack, and for the same reasons that National Guard armories—creno-lated like medieval fortresses—popped up on strategic sites in many American downtowns, so did government at all levels seem fatefully drawn to the architecture of Rome, seat of the most

9. George B. Post, Wisconsin Capitol Building (1904), Madison. *Photo by Robert Twombly*

10. McKim, Mead & White, Waiting Room, Pennsylvania Station (1902–10), New York. *Courtesy The Art Institute, Chicago*

enduring Western empire, in fact and in memory. The implication was, though hardly ever publicly proclaimed, that physical assault against the state or the private entities it chose to protect, and political assault on republican principles and forms of governance, would not prevail. Thus in the face of social upheaval and to announce its imperial objectives, numerous government buildings referred to those of the "eternal city."

Privately endowed quasi-public edifices served another imperialism: the desire of the owning caste to control the urban environment, physically and ideologically, which can be understood as a collective insertion of personal and entrepreneurial aspirations into the public realm. The great railway terminals—the Grand Centrals in New York and Chicago, the Union Stations in St. Louis, Pittsburgh, and Washington, D.C.—were strategic in this regard because they stood as introductions, as literally the first things travelers saw on arrival, becoming icons of their cities, prototypical edifices, in the same way the Transamerica Building today stands for San Francisco, the Renaissance Center for Detroit, and Peachtree Center for Atlanta. The terminals' indispensability, exceptional visibility, and key locations gave their owners unrivaled opportunities to make sweeping public pronouncements.

In McKim, Mead & White's neoclassical Pennsylvania Station (1902–10) in New York, the vast waiting room (fig. 10) was 25 percent larger than the gigantic tepidarium in the Roman Baths of Caracalla after which it was modeled. By exaggerating in scale this already obvious historical reference, the architects performed several important services for their clients, led by Alexander Johnston Cassatt; they helped make palatable corporate colonization of a huge parcel of prime New York real estate, confirming its control over a significant measure of public space in that a station is public in function and its construction required eliminating public thoroughfare; and they made their clients urban benefactors and icons, associating them with an age-old monument of art. In one fell swoop the Pennsylvania Railroad by its architectural decisions irrevocably changed the city's physical configuration and elevated its own cultural and civic standing.

In 1901 it took congressional action to remove a railroad terminal from the Washington Mall, which makes the implication of Pennsylvania Station all the more clear: the elite ordered public space for its own purposes. Its program certainly included, but was hardly restricted to, commercial gain, which becomes especially obvious when considering what is now called "cultural philanthropy." The late-nineteenth–early-twentieth-century proliferation of vast new buildings for museums, libraries, historical societies, opera companies, symphony orchestras, and universities, more often than not in Beaux Arts or neoclassical dress, occurred in every U.S. city of real or pretended standing coast to coast, sometimes in planned "civic center" clusters like Cleveland's and San Francisco's facing formal gardens. All had specific programs that were not so much sinister as class-determined: to decide which art and knowledge was legitimate and which was not, to limit access and instruction to acceptable individuals, to determine who would define, protect, and extend the cultural heritage.

Architectural strategies for achieving these objectives reinforced non-architectural. On the one hand, Chicago symphony and opera companies might refuse to perform German music in a vain attempt to perpetuate cultural control by Eastern-rooted Yankee families, and along with sister institutions elsewhere close their facilities after working hours and on weekends to exclude undesirables; on the other hand, stairwells, vestibules, corridors, and other spaces were made as monumental and impressive as possible, both to intimidate the unwanted who might slip in and to instill in everyone acceptance of what was deemed proper art and culture, including the building itself. Imposing façades and palace-like interiors of establishments like the Metropolitan, Boston, and Milwaukee museums of art were additionally intended to demonstrate the expertise, connoisseurship, and refined taste and thus validate the social standing of those responsible for erecting them, whether patrons (whose own collections further confirmed their status) or their architects.

The architects of culturally philanthropic edifices for the public realm were, of course, also the architects of châteaux and palazzi for private consumption (and in financial and social terms they benefited mightily). If, on the one hand, elaborate mansions signaled an individual's arrival in the aristocracy of wealth, on the other hand railroad terminals, cultural palaces, and the like spoke to that aristocracy's determination to "re-make the urban space if they so willed," in Lauro Martines's words: either in its entirety —witness the many proposals like Burnham's 1909 "Plan of Chicago" sponsored not by the city but by the elite Commercial Club

11. Daniel H. Burnham, Proposed Civic Center (1909), Chicago. *From Daniel H. Burnham and Edward H. Bennett,* Plan of Chicago, *edited by Charles Moore*

(fig. 11)—or piecemeal, project by civic project, mostly in that imperial style so well known that in 1912 Burnham did not need to identify it when instructing the Chamber of Commerce that in order to implement its plan for Brooklyn it would need to convince the public "that it pays in dollars and cents that their city should be beautiful." That republican governments by and large settled on the same imperial style indicates, perhaps, a certain agreement on its usefulness.

THE SKYSCRAPER AS
ICON, 1890–1920

DESPITE THE IMPORTANCE of buildings thus far discussed, none raised the architectural problems posed by the skyscraper. During the 1950s and 1960s historians wasted considerable effort defining and categorizing skyscrapers and attempting to identify the first one. All the layperson—and the expert, for that matter —needs to know is that they rise noticeably higher than the norm of their built surroundings, which meant they were approaching twenty stories in 1900 when the great majority were devoted to office space. At that time skyscrapers were ordinarily designed in one or more historical foreign styles even though they originated in the United States to accommodate new activity in certain sectors of the labor force: an exponential increase of clerical workers, significant growth of industrially based managers (and owners), and of their dependent professional and commercial purveyors. This meant that skyscrapers were mostly of two types: those intended primarily as rental properties built by realty developers or speculators, and those intended primarily as headquarters for large companies erected by entrepreneurs or by corporate owners. This division was the general rule, but there were exceptions.

Skyscrapers were massive urban intrusions, rising higher almost every year—in New York, Ernest Flagg's Singer Building reached forty-seven stories in 1908, Cass Gilbert's Woolworth fifty-five in 1913—and were beginning to absorb entire blocks. Realizing their threat to outstrip human capacity to comprehend—let alone see —them in their entirety, owners and architects placed banks and shops at ground level, while elaborately ornamenting entrances, lobbies, façades, and rooflines to catch the eye (and to advertise self and product). Owners also gave considerable attention to names. For company headquarters the choice was easy: Singer, Woolworth, Wrigley, or McCormick if individually owned; Metropolitan, Guaranty, Tribune, or Equitable if erected by a corporation. In the first case, at least, anthropomorphism brought the impersonal to life.

Builders of rental facilities had to be more imaginative, in Chicago, to take one example, mythologizing history to create an iconography of progress: the Marquette Building referred to an early French explorer, a priest; the Manhattan and the Virginia to areas of the country early Chicagoans had forsaken; the Montauk, Tacoma, Monadnock, Pontiac, and many others to Indian tribes (which were especially popular); the Rookery to pigeon roosts in temporary buildings formerly on the site. A brutal record was thus sanitized: God's brave European emissary opened the way for courageous settlers to remove the noble but obstructive savage in order to build a better world by improving the real estate. With the locality tamed by heroic effort, past and present became a harmonious continuity of inevitable improvement, and the skyscraper its domesticating agent. But to accept its civilizing importance—and at first many were reluctant for fear of height, fire, congestion, mechanical failure, inadequate light, and loss of commercial identity—was also to accept the corporatization and centralization of its big-business builders during an unprecedented period of mergers in the 1890s at the very moment the word "skyscraper" entered the language. Business consolidation, progress, and the tall building were thus conflated. By 1900 the skyscraper was seen as the prototypical American edifice, and its proliferation as a measure of national achievement. Which is what made it a difficult problem for architects.

How to turn this new building type into architecture was not obvious. Everyone agreed that "this sterile pile, this crude, harsh, brutal agglomeration, this stark, staring exclamation of eternal strife," as Louis Sullivan put it, was potentially a work of art, for skyscrapers were, after all, the possessions and workplaces of cultural and residential palace builders. But few agreed on the form the art should take. The most conservative approach was to design the tall building as though not tall at all, and two ways to do this were either to wrap every two or three floors with a heavy cornice or entablature so that the result resembled a stack of small identical structures (fig. 12) or to divide the façade into four or five units

12. George B. Post, St. Paul Building (1898–99), New York. *Courtesy Museum of the City of New York*

13. Benjamin Wistam Morris, Bank of New York and Trust Company (1927), New York. *From The New York Edison Company,* Towers of Manhattan. *Drawing by E. H. Suydam*

of different architectural treatment so that the result resembled a stack of small dissimilar structures (fig. 13). Architects of more literal bent rummaged around in history for adaptable building types: the campanile (fig. 14), the classical column (fig. 15), and the Gothic cathedral (fig. 16) were popular.

These approaches shared two characteristics: they associated the modern with the ancient by dressing the new genre in old clothing—reflecting the belief of most architects that design should change only incrementally, and then always remain close to historical precedent, which also suited the aesthetic inclinations of owners—and they ignored the implications of steel with which all skyscrapers were constructed by 1900. This was certainly true in New York, where high-rises were ordinarily treated in historical terms, but less the case in Chicago, the other center of skyscraper production at the turn of the century, where a group of commercial architects now known as the "Chicago School" (c. 1885–1910) turned away from history, it has often been said, which is only partly true.

In general, the New York prototype, which included the tallest buildings in the world (fig. 17), featured a pyramid or cupola top on a narrowish tower rising from a solid block, more facing material than glass, and elaborate multicolored projecting ornament; it was articulated more often vertically than horizontally while only ambiguously revealing the steel frame's location. The representative Chicago skyscraper was an untowered, flat-roofed, open block (hollow or U-shaped) with more glass than facing material, decorated more restrainedly with flush ornament in the façade's color, and articulated horizontally as emphatically as it was vertically, thus following and openly revealing the location of the frame. Louis Sullivan's inclination occasionally to disguise the frame by emphasizing only vertical members, and always to ornament his façades lavishly, was closer to mannerisms of his New York contemporaries than to his Chicago School colleagues, who, by and large, pursued their own courses until the two cities' skyscraper styles more or less merged in the early 1920s.

The so-called Chicago School never proclaimed a collective design philosophy based on shared principles, objectives, or *solidarité*, and in that sense was not a school at all. But it cannot be denied that the work of Holabird & Roche, Burnham & Root (later D. H. Burnham & Company), William Le Baron Jenney, Adler &

14. Napoleon LeBrun and Sons, Metropolitan Life Insurance Company (1909), New York. *From The New York Edison Company,* Towers of Manhattan. *Drawing by E. H. Suydam*

15. J. W. and M. J. Reid, Spreckles Building (1897), San Francisco. *From* American Architect and Building News, *1897*

16. Cass Gilbert, Woolworth Building (1911–14), New York. *Courtesy The Art Institute, Chicago*

17. Ernest Flagg, Singer Building (1906–8), New York. *From Francisco Mujica,* History of the Skyscraper

Sullivan, and several lesser firms bore a strong family resemblance. Their simplified façades responded to local conditions. The great fire of 1871 encouraged speedy, economical reconstruction with flame-retardant materials; spongy subsoil demanded lighter-weight structures. Steel resting on spread-footing or caisson foundations satisfied both needs, in addition permitting greater spans, hence more window space. Masonry gradually lost its load-bearing function to become skinlike infilling amid fenestration protecting against the elements, but as early as 1895 even that function was minimized by the nearly all-glass façade of Solon S. Bemen's Studebaker Building (fig. 18). The "great office and commercial buildings now found here" fulfilled "the business principles of real estate owners," compilers of the four-volume *Industrial Chicago* commented in 1891, which were that "light, space, air and strength were demanded . . . as the first objects and exterior ornamentation as the second." Five years later Montgomery Schuyler added that "in no other American city has commercial architecture become so exclusively utilitarian."

Industrial Chicago had nothing to say about *interior* ornamentation, but recent analysis suggests why it was as commonplace and lavish as elsewhere. Some of the reasons for ornamental richness are obvious: to impress transients and clients, to lend stature to owners, to advertise wares, to improve real estate value. Others are not so obvious: to instill company loyalty among employees, to engage in a kind of aesthetic competition with business rivals all the while differentiating one from another, and less obvious still, but perhaps most important, to add to the urban luster, to enhance civic pride. A perfect example of concealing interior lavishness behind restrained façades is Adler & Sullivan's 1886–90 Auditorium Building (figs. 19 and 20), where a massive, essentially unadorned granite exterior prepares one not at all for the incredibly ornate rooms within. This discrepancy, or rupture, between inside and out recalls the seventeenth-century bourgeois Dutch inclination in building matters to minimize public display of wealth, while the related notion that *interior* architectural activity was actually civic improvement further privatized a form of urban adornment carried over from *exteriors* of Quattrocento Florentine palazzi.

This rupture—utilitarian façades, elaborate interiors—made Chicago School architecture unique. The historically referential

18. Solon S. Bemen, Studebaker Brothers Building (1895), Chicago. *Courtesy The Art Institute, Chicago*

skyscraper façade common in New York extended into the business world the image of the owner as *l'homme d'art* established by residential and quasi-public structures. In Chicago, the extension was accomplished by interiors. These were the quasi-public spaces most closely associated with corporate and entrepreneurial owners by virtue of name identification, of the myriad daily activities—

waiting, meeting, and greeting, buying newspapers, escaping the
rain, making phone calls, getting haircuts, even using toilets—that
increasingly occurred therein, and because, by attaching the idea
of *civic* amenity to privately owned skyscraper interiors, owners
expanded the meaning of "public space," bringing it indoors, under closer control through direct supervision.

In Chicago, but not in New York, a "utilitarian" exterior defined
the owner as *homo economicus*. (Concern for employee health and
safety implied by the importance accorded in *Industrial Chicago*
to "light, space, air and strength" can thus be understood as primarily a matter of productivity.) Being rational and gridlike, and
so fundamentally similar, "utilitarian" façades were as visually neutral as the local plat map they would have resembled if laid on the
ground and made two-dimensional. The industrial and topograph-

19. Adler & Sullivan, Auditorium Building (1886–90), Chicago. *From* The Artistic Guide to Chicago and
the World's Columbian Exposition *(1892)*

20. Louis H. Sullivan, Hotel lobby in the Auditorium Building (1886–90), Chicago. *Photo provided by John Vinci*

ical iconography of each was thus the iconology of all because builders and owners had ceded to each other access to a common architectural language. In one way, the Chicago façade was socially neutral as well, revealing nothing about individual entrepreneurs and little about them collectively beyond group identification with efficiency, utility, modern technology, and business-like demeanor. Yet, when these very characteristics were put into architectural form with geometric and mechanical precision and blown up in scale—Chicago skyscrapers were generally wider than New York's in relation to height, giving the impression of great bulk—they were socially loaded in another way: as statements of massive strength and uncontested power. Compared to more conventionally detailed tall buildings, Chicago façades were abstractions detached from familiar historical and contemporary association; they were paeans to the "timelessness" of modern, rationalized production, asserting that the commercial values of the new elite had always existed, had always been preferable to others, and would always be the norm.

From the point of view of social relations, however, the Chicago rupture between inside and out was not a rupture at all, but a change in entrepreneurial strategy. *Homo economicus* was for general public consumption, *l'homme d'art* for those privy to privately controlled "public" spaces, that is, for "the better sort." The former signified a single, and rather hard-bitten, public image, the latter, a more complex, multifaceted, even reflective, personality that was heading indoors, seeking shelter from civic scrutiny. Here is the first architectural indication—it would be a fixture of post-World War II "modernism"—that the business elite would retreat behind anonymous walls, that its cultural and social intentions would be less obvious, that it would strut less conspicuously, that it would be more discreet.

It is unlikely that Chicago's business oligarchy was more prescient, socially responsible, well-intentioned or, conversely, more defensive than others. On the contrary, in a far-from-conquered physical and economic environment, in a place widely known as "the land of the dollars," with few social constraints on entrepreneurial behavior, local business barons were likely to be as short-sighted, socially irresponsible, ill-intentioned, and aggressive as others elsewhere. In such a climate, subtle suggestions of artistic refinement carried less visual weight than utilitarian proclamations of power and strength, which is what Chicago School façades were all about. The irony is that what was offered in the early 1900s as a kind of braggadocio was transformed by later generations into an emblem of cool detachment. Taken together, Chicago façades and interiors announced that a shift of social style was in the offing, and therein may lie their real modernity.

ALTERING HABITAT: NEW
AGENDAS FOR RESIDENTIAL
DESIGN, 1900–1940

FRANK LLOYD WRIGHT WAS a Chicago School product in that, while working for Adler & Sullivan from 1888 to 1893, he imbibed many of Sullivan's ideas, including one of particular moment that only he among his contemporaries made the operational basis of his work. Sullivan had argued that since the skyscraper had become the prototypical U.S. building, its proper façade expression could become the basis for a national architectural style. In some twenty or more built and unbuilt projects from 1890 to 1904, Sullivan developed two high-rise models: what he called a "system of vertical construction" emphasizing tallness (a structural interpretation of a visual characteristic: see fig. 21, the 1894 Guaranty Building in Buffalo) and what can be called a "system of skeletal construction" emphasizing the frame (a visual interpretation of a structural characteristic: see fig. 22, the 1898–1903 Schlesinger & Mayer, now Carson Pirie Scott, Store in Chicago). But like other Chicago School work, his "systems" had limited application since they addressed only exteriors for large-scale commercial operations. Except for Sullivan's and possibly John Root's work, which ended prematurely in 1891 with his death at age forty-one, the Chicago façade was motivated more by economics than by aesthetics. It was not the outcome of artistic impulses; nor was it the consequence of any fundamental cultural upheaval or intellectual reorganization. Chicago commercial architecture was less a style— even less the first indigenous or the first modern style, as many have claimed—than a mannered appliqué, like the neoclassic, for a self-serving plutocracy.

If Sullivan therefore failed in his mission, he certainly made a lasting impact on Wright, who took up his challenge. Like Sulli-

21. Adler & Sullivan, Guaranty Building (1894–95), Buffalo. *The Chicago Architectural Photographing Company*

22. Louis H. Sullivan, Schlesinger & Mayer (now Carson Pirie Scott) Store (1898, 1902–3), Chicago. *Courtesy Chicago Historical Society*

van's, but unlike the Chicago School's, Wright's *conscious* objective was to create a specifically "Usonian" (a word he later coined to refer to the United States of North America) aesthetic suitable for all architectural occasions, and to a remarkable extent he succeeded. Wright's first great achievement—called the "prairie house" (fig. 23) because its long, low, horizontal configuration interpreted characteristics of regional terrain—was the underpinning of a comprehensive "prairie style" in which he designed structures as diverse as churches, commercial buildings, schools, boathouses, mortuaries, garages, banks, real estate offices, art galleries and installations, hotels, dance academies, and horse fountains, indeed, anything for which he was commissioned. Aesthetically, stylistically, in each situation, his exterior, interior, landscaping, and furnishings were of a piece, conceived as an architectural whole. Rejecting the customary practice of reserving

23. Frank Lloyd Wright, "A Home in a Prairie Town." *From* the Ladies' Home Journal, *1901*

24. Frank Lloyd Wright, Hiram Baldwin residence (1905), Kenilworth, Illinois. *Photo by Robert Twombly*

particular styles for certain circumstances—like Gothic for churches, neoclassical for banks—and assembling patchwork quilts of interior spaces unrelated to exterior form, Wright's work was ahistorical and holistic. And because it confronted a social issue of national importance—the widely perceived predicament of the urban middle-class family—it was the closest the United States ever got to a homegrown style of its own.

Virtually unlimited stylistic applicability distinguished him from other architects—less so from his few dozen mostly Midwestern imitators collectively called the "prairie school"—but what distinguished him most was the nature of the work on which he concentrated. Historically, most elite architects are solely or best known for nonresidential buildings even when luxury dwellings are a substantial part of their corpus; even today, especially today, if they design private houses at all it is early in their careers before they are able to land more lucrative commissions. Wright was the first visible U.S. architect since the Civil War to make his reputation from private houses and the first ever to do it with dwellings not intended for the rich.

From 1901 when he announced the prairie house in the *Ladies' Home Journal* to roughly 1915 when as the first American architect of real international standing he somewhat abruptly changed direction in his work, Wright executed approximately 120 structures of which only 30 percent were nonresidential including only four that were and are well known: the Larkin Building (1904) in Buffalo; Unity Temple (1905–6) in Oak Park, Illinois; Midway Gardens (1913–14) in Chicago; and the Imperial Hotel (1913–22) in Tokyo. Even in the 1950s, when he was possibly the most visible architect in the world—designing the Guggenheim Museum, the "Mile High" skyscraper, the Marin County Civic Center, and whole districts of Baghdad—nonresidential work dropped to 20 percent of his built total. Wright became famous and remained famous throughout a seventy-two-year career primarily because of single-family suburban houses for the middle and upper-middle class.

It is no accident that one of his heroes was Thomas Jefferson, whose idealization of American yeomanry he took to heart. Wright believed that the sturdily independent, home-owning therefore landed, resourceful small businessman, professional, and manager—the backbone of the nation, he insisted—was the modern version of Jefferson's eighteenth-century paragon of virtue. The prairie house was a complete residential reconfiguration based on a considered examination of the contemporary "yeoman" family, which Wright elevated to a cultural icon, the repository of "Americanness" itself.

Since this family was imperiled, many observers thought, Wright set out to save it. The prairie house (fig. 24) literally encouraged and symbolically represented: closer association with the natural world lost to city dwellers; withdrawal from a threatening urban milieu into a visibly protective, visually inaccessible sanctuary; family togetherness stimulated by an open plan, orderliness stemming from highly structured spaces; and psychic serenity deriving from holistic design. This amalgam of memory and desire—personal peace stemming from family harmony in a safe, nurturing retreat wedded to nature—was intended to reassure anxious middle-class urbanites by recalling the happier if mythical small towns and rural areas that they, their parents, or grandparents had left. If prairie house reality and representation called to mind idyllic country chapels like the one in Wisconsin he had helped his family construct as a boy, it is because Wright had turned the middle-class dwelling into a sacramental place, a kind of shrine of traditional family values. But if its social orientation faced the past, its aesthetics pointed uncompromisingly to the future, for they were daringly new, considered "radical" and disturbing even by intelligent culture critics like Chicago's Harriet Monroe. Wright's genius was to resolve this contradiction and to sell it to fundamentally conservative clients. In so doing, he bonded avant-garde art to the rise of the middle class.

Wright's achievement had profound implications for the social relations of his profession. He extended the acceptable range of elite architectural activity downward into the middle class. He opened new avenues to visibility for architects who might not have attained it otherwise and helped solidify the social position of all visible architects by expanding their possibilities for social usefulness. He delivered to them a new client pool by elevating its architectural requirements to fine art. And since that art was on the cutting edge, making serious waves in Europe as early as 1910, he forced the American "academy," so to speak, to reckon with dissent. None of this happened overnight, and Wright did not act alone, but he was the principal player, and after his performance there was no going back.

Throughout all this and more vehemently as he grew older, Wright remained a professional loner, thumbing his nose—figuratively and almost literally—at elite colleagues who came so to hate him that their premier organization, the American Institute of Architects, withheld from him its gold medal for life achievement until 1949 when he was eighty-two, long after it had honored many younger and lesser practitioners and long after it already owed him a huge debt of gratitude.

Principally because of Wright, middle- to upper-middle-class housing acquired artistic visibility before World War I. But he was not the only stylistic innovator. Some of his prairie-school followers produced striking if derivative work, particularly the husband and wife team of Walter Burley Griffin and Marion Mahony (the first female graduate of MIT), Barry Byrne (later excelling in ecclesiastical work), and the firm of George Grant Elmslie and William Purcell. Others far removed from Wright's direct influence were developing their own original vocabularies, especially in California. In Pasadena, the brothers Charles S. and Henry M. Greene applied Japanese joinery techniques to the asymmetrical stone and wood "stick" and "shingle" styles of previous decades, and to Gustav Stickley's work, creating a series of stunning houses resembling Wright's at a distance but in fact artistically distinctive (fig. 25). And in San Diego, Irving Gill combined the Spanish heritage, experiments in concrete prefabrication and in stucco, and his own geometrical ornament into clean-lined, smooth-surfaced compositions for all classes of families that sometimes eerily anticipated the so-called international style of the 1920s (fig. 26).

With clients from the rising middle class increasingly available, aspiring and elite architects gave them greater attention, so that in the interwar years middle-class housing became a major focus. Artistic innovation flagged, however, as visible practitioners moved into the field. Even during the prairie school's heyday (which coincided with Gill's and the Greenes'), traditional architecture had been the overwhelming choice: the style of almost all middle-class dwellings had been modest versions of elite preferences. But during the 1920s especially, stylistic progressivism was even less evident.

There are several reasons for this. Personal difficulties temporarily removed Wright from a leadership role, and most of his followers drifted away. As visible architects appropriated middle-

25. Charles S. and Henry M. Greene, David B. Gamble residence (1908), Pasadena, California. *Photo by Robert Twombly*

26. Irving Gill, Walter L. Dodge residence (1914–16), West Hollywood, California. *Photo by Marvin Rand*

class housing, furthermore, their inclination to stick with the familiar was if anything welcomed by aspiring, upwardly mobile clients happy to take artistic cues from the very rich. (Never in their wildest dreams could the 1880s and 1890s sponsors and agents of elite cultural hegemony have imagined how easy their triumph would be.) Then, too, more U.S. architects were training at the École des Beaux-Arts and its American derivatives, all bastions of design conservatism. In addition, decades of imperial adventures and internal unrest had created a kind of yearning in certain circles for a supposedly simple and untroubled past; this stimulated withdrawals into nostalgic regionalisms that had made an early mark with the "local color" literary movement and then with architectural revivals, first of New England and Southern "colonial," later of Spanish, that peaked in the 1920s. U.S. participation in World War I also played a role, bringing Allied architectural traditions to a wider American audience through eye-witnesses and photographs, especially English Tudor, which was immensely popular prior to the Depression. Finally, as middle-class housing groups and planned communities, including the garden variety, sprang up around the nation between 1910 and 1930, corporate, trade union, charitable, and plain old speculative developers saw little reason to go out on artistic limbs.

Sponsors of residential developments had diverse motives. But neither housing reformers, labor organizations, speculators, nor municipal officials thought stylistic experimentation would have much appeal. The tried and true was better, more marketable than the new design ideas beginning to arrive from Europe, which some, on the heels of the postwar "red scare," thought to be artistic "un-American" activities. Other kinds of experiments there most certainly were, however: in separating vehicular from pedestrian traffic and in garaging automobiles, in cooperative financing and ownership, in communal space provision (play areas, gardens, meeting rooms), in internal circulation, the handling of town centers, the arrangement of both attached and detached housing on irregular and superblocks, and so on and on depending upon the project. Because of these and many other appealing provisions, the 1920s were something of a "golden age" for multiple housing in the United States. Not before nor since were so many handsome, affordable, well constructed, and still desirable units erected for middle-class residents replete with design lessons, furthermore, that are still applicable today regardless of income level.

But stylistically there was little new and little to be built upon. Some of the best known undertakings are Grosvenor Atterbury's Forest Hills Gardens (1909–13) in Queens, New York, sponsored by the Russell Sage Foundation in English Tudor; Howard Van Doren Shaw's Market Square (1913) with an Austrian village look for the Lake Forest (Illinois) Improvement Association; Bertram Grosvenor Goodhue's Spanish revival Tyrone, New Mexico (1914), for the Phelps–Dodge Company; Henry Wright and Clarence S. Stein's Sunnyside Gardens (1924–29), Queens, financed by Manhattan investors; and their town of Radburn, New Jersey (1928–29), financed by its residents, the first (fig. 27) in a kind of friendly mill style, the second vaguely New England colonial. Stein and Wright were political progressives, members of the Regional Planning Association, hoping to build a sense of collectivity in self-sufficient communities. Atterbury cultivated his reputation as a social progressive through his work for the Russell Sage Foundation (founded in 1907 for "the improvement of social and living conditions") but he was also quite comfortable designing country estates. Goodhue was an eclectic attempting to update one or another historical style depending upon the commission. Shaw flirted briefly with the prairie style but preferred medieval mannerisms. Regardless of the political or aesthetic inclinations of its architects, in other words, collective housing—almost all privately financed, it should be noted—was stylistically retrograde or at best tentative. Along with contemporary individual dwellings, it indicates a period of treading water during which elite architects tightened a grip on middle-class architectural production that would ease only after World War II.

By that time, due to the economic crisis of the 1930s, some states, but especially the federal government, had built a certain amount of social—in the United States, public—housing. Because one-third of the 15 million unemployed in 1933 had worked in the building trades, New Deal policy had a dual objective: to create jobs by renewing the housing stock. Against tremendous opposition from the real estate lobby, the Subsistence Homestead Division of the National Industrial Recovery Administration constructed agricultural and industrial workers' colonies, Hightstown, New Jersey, and the Arthursdale project at Reedsville, West Virginia, being the best known, while the Farm Security Administration improved conditions at more than thirty migrant labor camps for some 15,000

27. Clarence S. Stein and Henry Wright, Sunnyside Gardens (1924–29), Queens, New York. *From Stein,* Toward New Towns in America

28. Douglas D. Ellington and R. J. Wadsworth, chief architects, and Hale Walker, town planner, Greenbelt, Maryland (1935–41). *Photo by Fairchild Aerial Surveys, courtesy Library of Congress*

families in addition to building other rural housing. The Resettlement Administration's most famous undertaking was the planning and construction of three suburban towns: Greenbelt, Maryland (fig. 28), Greendale, Wisconsin, and Greenhills, Ohio, outside Washington, D.C., Milwaukee, and Cincinnati, respectively. Of the ninety-nine residential communities built under New Deal auspices, forty were rural or suburban, and like the privately sponsored ventures of the 1920s were, on the whole, stylistically conservative.

The Public Works Administration (PWA), on the other hand, concentrated on slum clearance and low-rent urban housing, but was able to build only forty-nine projects with 25,000 dwelling units between 1933 and 1937. Because some were of conspicuously better quality than most privately built workers' residences, PWA projects aroused strong political opposition. Since some—like the Carl Mackley Houses in Philadelphia—included tennis courts, swimming pools, libraries, laundries, and nurseries (facilities usually associated with middle-income living); and others—like the Williamsburg Houses in New York—hired out-of-work sculptors, ceramicists, and master masons to produce beautiful friezes, handsome tiled hallways, and elaborate brickwork; and since still others offered good-quality modern appliances, realtors claimed that tenancy was "so attractive that the urge to buy one's own home will be diminished." Consequently, the Wagner-Steagall Housing Act of 1937 shifted responsibility for residential construction to the new U.S. Housing Authority (USHA), which, in contrast to its predecessor, produced fourteen times as many projects (some 350)—albeit with only four times as many units (under 100,000) —during a comparable three-and-one-half-year period ending in 1940. But the shift in responsibility, while erecting more apartments, also meant diminished amenity.

PWA housing, after all, had been built for the so-called deserving poor, that is, for those who, it was said, had always worked hard, were only temporarily down and out through no fault of their own, and would likely purchase a house someday. USHA projects, on the other hand, were intended for the "very poor," an admirable objective that also meant "no frills" construction. PWA's occasional experiments with solar heating, with regional building traditions (Spanish stucco style in the Southwest, French wrought-iron railings in New Orleans), with new materials like glass brick, social services like day care and community rooms, and with giving a free hand to skilled artisans, was supplanted by USHA's cheaper materials, lower budgets, and comparatively unimaginative designs. The projects were, to be sure, sturdily constructed, intelligently laid out, and more congenial than poor people were used to. But they were also visually and practically less pleasing: no doors, in some instances, on kitchen cabinets and closets, entryways too small to store bicycles, plasterboard as opposed to plaster walls, linoleum on plywood rather than hardwood floors, and the like, the idea being that the very poor were best served by being discouraged from settling in, made to feel that if only they worked harder at pulling themselves up by their own bootstraps they, like their "deserving" brethren, might also "move up and out" to private-sector apartments off the "dole." And unlike PWA housing, that of USHA was not owned and operated by the federal government, but was built and run by local authorities with federal loans and guidelines, meaning discrepancies in quality control and provision of services depending upon region and the racial composition of tenants. Realtors were somewhat placated by this 1937 policy shift but continued to insist that public housing sapped individual initiative, destroyed self-reliance, and, worst of all, led to socialism.

Compared to state and municipally sponsored social housing in pre- and postwar Europe, 1930s public housing in the United States suffered in quantity and often in quality. But the fact remains that New Deal projects and those in a handful of states represented the first concerted attempt in national history to provide decent dwelling for the millions of poor people who were not and cannot be adequately served by the marketplace. They also set a precedent for the vastly larger "urban renewal" housing campaigns in the post-World War II era, especially during the 1950s and 1960s. But like the architecture of that more recent period, and of the 1920s, New Deal dwellings were, by and large, stylistically uninspiring, hardly surprising in the United States, considering the population for whom they were erected.

THE SOCIAL
TRANSFORMATION OF
MODERNISM, 1922–1940

THERE HAD BEEN, however, tiny rivulets of avant-garde architectural activity in the United States during the 1920s, but they were far removed socially from public housing. One rivulet came from Wright—less from his work, since he was designing little at the time and that a rather exotic dead end, than from his continued call for an indigenous national architecture. Another came from among the 259 entries from around the world to the 1922 competition for new *Chicago Tribune* headquarters. A third resulted from the arrival of young Europeans, particularly Richard Neutra and Rudolph Schindler from Vienna and William Lescaze from Zurich. And the fourth, the source of the second and third, was the gradual but inexorable penetration of the United States by new European architecture, which in quantity of production was mostly social housing. Centered in Germany, Austria, The Netherlands, and France, "modernism," so-called, was tentatively taken up during the decade by a handful of visible architects who had previously designed in historic styles. In residential work it would make its great impact after World War II, but in commercial architecture it made a significant if limited mark before the Depression shut down building activity. By then it had helped point in a new direction the stylistic unification of New York and Chicago that had already occurred early in the 1920s.

The *Chicago Tribune* competition had contradictory but profound consequences for U.S. architecture. On the one hand, its winning neo-Gothic design administered the coup de grâce to the Chicago School, but on the other hand it compelled U.S. practitioners to cope with the new European work. The *Tribune* competition was a major architectural event, like the 1990s J. Paul

Getty Center in Santa Monica, California, "the commission of the century" of its day, offering the winner not only the most important local undertaking since the Auditorium Building of the 1880s but also international notoriety. The winners were John Mead Howells and Raymond Hood (the principal designer), who produced and built (from 1923 to 1925) a New York tower in Gothic akin to Cass Gilbert's Woolworth Building of 1911 to 1914 (compare fig. 29 to fig. 16). It had familiar Chicago features, to be sure: its base, shaft, and crown were clearly distinguished. But it was not a build-ing to sit comfortably with its "utilitarian" neighbors that had set the local tone, although it would have sat comfortably in lower Manhattan. Had the competition not been so highly touted, the entries so closely scrutinized, and the architects so widely ac-claimed, Tribune Tower might have quietly found its place in the downtown architectural jumble. But its symbolic and corporate visibility made that impossible, and it was important enough to be a national bellwether. Since it was inevitably and correctly com-pared to its parent structure, the Woolworth, still the world's tallest building and already legendary, it told the architecturally literate that the winds had changed, that the Chicago School had suc-cumbed to the New York style.

But if anyone in Gotham thought to claim a hometown victory, he would have been ill-advised, for the winds were swirling un-predictably. Other competition entries were much more to be reckoned with, in both the long and not-so-long run. Not that Tribune Tower was immediately forgettable; on the contrary, it remains one of the most handsome, best executed buildings of its kind, a landmark of its city and of "traditionalist" high-rise design. But even before it was finished it was artistically out of date.

Both the Gothic tower and the New York style were abandoned by Hood in his very next important building, in 1924 for the American Radiator Company (fig. 30) in New York, closely mod-eled after the competition's second-place winner by Finland's Eliel Saarinen. Saarinen combined new ideas with old (fig. 31). His vertically emphasized columns were Gothic-inspired but most of his arches were Romanesque, his sculptures would soon be called Art Deco and, most important, his setbacks were soaring extensions of traditional and contemporary European work (at the time that of Henri Sauvage in Paris, for example), which diminished grad-ually in mass upward through five recessions to the top. This was

29. Raymond Hood (with John Mead Howells), Chicago Tribune Building (1922–25). *From* The international competition for a new administration building for the Chicago tribune, MCMXXII . . . *(Chicago, c. 1923). Courtesy The Art Institute, Chicago*

30. Raymond Hood, American Radiator Building (1924), New York. *From The New York Edison Company*, Towers of Manhattan. *Drawing by Harley D. Nichols*

31. Eliel Saarinen, second prize entry (1922). *From* The international competition for a new administration building for the Chicago tribune, MCMXXII . . . *(Chicago, c. 1923). Courtesy The Art Institute, Chicago*

neither the Chicago nor the New York solution for handling a high-rise crown. Architect Claude Bragdon called the effect a "frozen fountain," and even before it became a staple in such books as architectural renderer Hugh Ferriss's *Metropolis of Tomorrow* (1929) it was being built as the towering ziggurat. Soon, with new ornamental treatment, the more fully developed and closely related Art Deco and "streamline" or "American moderne" styles—Art Deco was a vertical architecture in polychrome with rectilinear and zigzag ornament, moderne horizontal with curved surfaces, particularly at corners, and contrasting trim substituting for applied ornament—were dominating new construction. By the late 1920s and early 1930s in New York, the Daily News, Newsweek, Chanin, Chrysler, and Empire State buildings, 500 Fifth Avenue, and Rockefeller Center were variations on their and Saarinen's themes. But so too were Trost and Trost's 1928 Luhrs Tower in Phoenix, John R. and Donald Parkinson's Bullock's Wilshire Department Store (fig. 32) in Los Angeles the same year, Holabird & Root's 1929–30 Chicago Board of Trade, and tall buildings everywhere else.

Art Deco and moderne were the first and rather tepid U.S. responses to European modernism, but their superordinancy was almost as short-lived as the Tribune Tower's Gothic victory, partly because the Depression ended almost all large-scale commercial construction, and partly because other competition entries, unlike Saarinen's, were radical rejections of the architectural past, proving to have more lasting import. In their book accompanying a 1932 retrospective at the new Museum of Modern Art in New York, historian Henry-Russell Hitchcock and architectural curator Philip Johnson labeled those rejections since 1922 the "international style," a misnomer based on the misconception that quite different work from several nations and architects could be subsumed under one rubric. But the name stuck, probably because of visual similarities regardless of locale or designer.

In general, the new European architecture (fig. 33) replaced applied ornament with what can be called self-decoration: the composition resulting from the organization for visual effect of structural members, wall openings, and other requisites like downspouts, railings, terraces, and overhanging roofs. Long runs of ribbon windows flush with smooth, taut, skinlike walls were conceived as parts of the surface, not as holes in it. Roofs were flat, color was usually monochromatic (often white), major façade components were organized asymmetrically, and the construction was mostly skeletal. Form and material emphasized volume rather than mass, that is, interior spaciousness linked to outdoors as opposed to stalwart exteriors keeping outdoors at bay. These aspects of European social and private housing, schools, factories, and shops were just making their presence felt in 1922 and, except for rare instances (such as early proposals by Mies van der Rohe), were not applied to skyscrapers (which were even rarer in Europe at the time). But the artistic vocabularies were there, and the *Tribune* competition seems to have stimulated their application to tall buildings, which, in turn, influenced the only two international-style high-rises in the United States before World War II.

Less dramatic but the more visually consistent of the two was

32. John R. and Donald Parkinson, Bullock's Wilshire Department Store (1928), Los Angeles.
Photo by Julius Shulman

33. Corbusier, Villa Savoye (1929–31), Poissy, France. *Photo by Robert Twombly*

the 1929–31 McGraw-Hill Building (fig. 34) in New York, the result of Raymond Hood's latest stylistic transformation, which seems to have been influenced by Hans and Wassili Luckhardt and Alfons Anker, a trio of German modernists who submitted their *Tribune* entry anonymously. The Luckhardt–Anker scheme (fig. 35) featured three window tiers encased by four finlike projections climbing uninterruptedly from sidewalk to roof where, with a moderne curve, they folded rearward to act as projecting eaves for a series of setbacks. This bold façade stripe was flanked by horizontally articulated floors, each with a band of continuous windows. Except for a conspicuously offset corner, Hood retained the Germans' symmetrical organization, flattening their central stripe and flanking horizontals while lengthening their setbacks to achieve a more towered and thinner-skinned composition. Hood revealed the frame in back with a simply stated masonry grid but on the other façades subordinated it to vivid green-brick horizontal banding and runs of ribbon windows, although the front central stripe indicating interior vertical circulation also reflected the frame's vertical properties. From a distance, however, and in certain lights, McGraw-Hill appeared encircled bottom to top by ring upon ring of glass and brick, a study in horizontality unlike anything else in New York (or in any other city). It was as different from

William Van Alen's Art Deco Chrysler Building (1926–30) rising simultaneously down the street as Luckhardt-Anker's project was from the Woolworth.

More dramatic but less visually consistent was William Lescaze's (and George Howe's) Philadelphia Savings Fund Society (PSFS) Building (fig. 36) of 1929–32, which referred to the *Tribune* entry by Danish architect Knud Lönberg-Holm, itself based on Dutch de Stijl, with boldly contrasting color fields, sharp edges, minimalist detailing, powerful asymmetry, and oversized graphics. PSFS had

34. Raymond Hood (with André Fouilhoux), McGraw-Hill Building (1929–31), New York. *Photo by Robert Twombly*

35. Hans and Wassili Luckhardt and Alfons Anker, anonymously submitted entry (1922). *From* The international competition for a new administration building for the Chicago tribune, MCMXXII . . . *(Chicago, c. 1923). Courtesy The Art Institute, Chicago*

36. William Lescaze (with George Howe), Philadelphia Savings Fund Society
Building (1929–32), Philadelphia. *Courtesy The Library Company of Philadelphia*

all this, including the graphics. But in addition its upper stories
were slightly cantilevered, its two-story banking mezzanine was
sheathed in glass, and its penthouse dining room was roofed with
a projecting slab that in a de Stijlian gesture fired into the building's
core an arrow of color complementing that of the vertical rear
spine. Some exterior walls were horizontal, others vertical, still
others both. From every viewing angle, PSFS made a different
statement. Like McGraw-Hill, it was a startlingly new example of
structure determining appearance.

Perhaps more important in the long run than the Luckhardt-
Anker or Lönberg-Holm entries, however, or even Hood's and
Lescaze's interpretations of them, was the *Tribune* proposal (fig.
37) by Walter Gropius, director of the Bauhaus design school in
Weimar, Germany. Gropius dramatized the frame as no one in
the United States ever had, using the configuration of its structural
members, their glass infilling, and cantilevered and recessed terraces as his compositional scheme. His roofs were flat, his "Chicago
windows"—broad glass plates flanked by sash—were numerous
and almost flush with the surface. The overall image was of a

37. Walter Gropius (with Adolf Meyer), entry (1922). *From* The international competition for a new administration building for the Chicago tribune, MCMXXII . . . *(Chicago, c. 1923). Courtesy The Art Institute, Chicago*

pristine, hard-edged, machine-like edifice stripped of anything inessential. Along with entries by Berliners Max Taut and Ludwig Hilberseimer, and other Europeans discussed above, Gropius explored Chicago School implications that U.S. architects had not yet absorbed. After his proposal was digested, and quickly it was, Art Deco and moderne, even McGraw-Hill and PSFS, became footnotes to history as "modern" began to rewrite its pages.

Outside the high-rise genre, Rudolph Schindler and Richard Neutra produced the best known early international-style buildings in the United States. Both worked briefly with Wright between arriving from Vienna and settling permanently in Los Angeles. Schindler's oceanside "Health House" (1925–26; fig. 38) for Dr. Philip Lovell in Newport Beach, California, combined aspects of de Stijl, Soviet constructivism, and internationalism in two large concrete volumes—one for bedrooms, the other for living areas —raised above the sand on five poured-concrete frames. A year later for the same client, Neutra lifted a glassy, steel-framed, cantilever-terraced residence (fig. 39) from its hilly Los Angeles site on the kind of slender *pilotis* so favored by Corbusier. Neutra's design quickly became a landmark of U.S. modernism while Schindler's was neglected for years, apparently because it was thought too massive to represent the new, volumetric look.

Lescaze's other work—private residences for wealthy clients, unbuilt public-housing proposals, commercial and cultural structures—remained firmly in the international style throughout the 1930s. Hood, too, dabbled in it off and on until his death in 1934. Elsewhere, Albert Frey and A. Lawrence Kochner on Long Island, George F. and William Keck in Chicago, Gregory Ain and Ralph S. Soriano in California, as well as Neutra and Schindler and a few other architects around the nation embraced the new style. But it was the arrival in 1937 of three Germans fleeing Nazism that gave great momentum to modernism here. Walter Gropius became a professor at Harvard School of Design, collaborating with his former Bauhaus colleague Marcel Breuer until Breuer opened his own office in 1940. Breuer remained active until his death in 1981, specializing in modernist houses, but shifting his vocabulary somewhat to accommodate new stylistic currents in the 1960s, especially for nonresidential work. Mies van der Rohe, who always remained faithful to his initial artistic inspiration, became director of the Architecture Department at the newly reorganized Illinois Institute of Technology (IIT) in 1938 and immediately

38. Rudolph Schindler, Philip Lovell residence ("Health House," 1929), New-port Beach, California. *From David Gebhard and Robert Winter,* A Guide to Architecture in Southern California

39. Richard Neutra, Philip Lovell residence (1927–29), Los Angeles. *Courtesy The Art Institute, Chicago*

began designing its campus. From their secure academic bastions, Gropius and Mies broadcast modernism for the next thirty years, training legions of students while influencing legions more at other institutions. By the end of the 1930s, while modernism was atrophying in Europe, partly because it had run its course and partly because of official opposition in Germany and the Soviet Union, it was securing a strong foothold in the United States.

There were two other important developments during the 1930s. With a series of stunning designs from 1935 to 1938 Wright reappeared as a forceful presence. His "Fallingwater" weekend house (1935–36) for Edgar J. Kaufmann near Pittsburgh—considered by many the finest private dwelling of this century—translated modernist vocabulary into his own "organic" language (fig. 40): myriad pieces of rough fieldstone, tiny metal frames, and small glass panels wedded to daringly cantilevered concrete terraces were attached so seamlessly over a waterfall to the hillside that the house became a reconstruction, an extension, an interpretation of, and a tribute to its site. Few other buildings in the history of architecture were so much a part of their surroundings, so "organic," Wright would have said. Fallingwater was undoubtedly a tour de force, and very likely a calculated rebuttal to those younger architects—Wright turned seventy in 1937—who had pronounced his work passé during the previous decade. Then in 1936 came the Johnson Wax Administration Building in Racine, Wisconsin, possibly the finest of all moderne work of the period, and the Herbert Jacobs residence in Madison, Wisconsin, the first of his modestly priced, partially prefabricated "Usonian" houses for middle-class clients, with wide-open floor plans, huge sheets of glass, flat overhanging roofs, and in-floor heating. In 1937 there was "Wingspread," a luxury residence for the president of Johnson Wax, and in 1938 Wright's own "Taliesin West" complex near Scottsdale, Arizona, as well as the first of several buildings for Florida Southern College in Lakeland.

In its strict adherence to basic geometries, its rectilinearity in many cases, its occasional use of steel and concrete, its horizontality, its diminished ornamentation, and its asymmetry, Wright's new work resembled the Europeans' by which it was surely influenced (although none of these characteristics were new to him), giving it a more "contemporary" look. But in its use of "natural" materials—Wright preferred unpainted wood, brick, glass, and

40. Frank Lloyd Wright, Edgar J. Kaufmann residence ("Fallingwater," 1935–36), Bear Run, Pennsylvania. *Photo by Robert Twombly*

undressed stone—and therefore in color, in its greater openness to the outdoors, its unmatched site specificity, and its equally unmatched exploitation of environmental factors for cooling and heating, his work was distinctly his own. He liked to say it was "modern" but not "modernistic," and indeed it certainly was idiosyncratic.

Even so, his earlier work was included in the 1932 Museum of Modern Art "Modern Architecture—International Exhibition" which was—more than Wright's return, more than Gropius's and Mies's arrival, more than the increasing sorties into internationalism—the most significant architectural event of the decade because it heralded the elite's appropriation of modernism as its own—not Wright's modernism, of course, but that of the international style.

The exhibition, which has become legendary in architectural annals, was divided into three parts. Section 1, "Modern Architects," featured four Europeans (Corbusier from France, J.J.P. Oud from The Netherlands, Gropius and Mies from Germany) and five Americans (Wright, Howe & Lescaze, Hood, Neutra, and the Bowman brothers, who are nearly forgotten today but were reasonably well known at the time). According to the exhibition's historian, Section 1 was "heavily skewed toward single-family house's [sic] and school projects." And that is certainly true. Of the forty-three individual or multiple building projects depicted, only four—two by Oud, one each by Gropius and Lescaze—qualify as social or public housing. Section 2, "The Extent of Modern Architecture," contained forty projects by thirty-seven architects (six American) from fifteen countries. Only four were multiple housing, including one for professional women and another for senior citizens; none could be defined as social housing—publicly or collectively financed for working people—in the European sense of the term.

Section 3, "Housing," featured four projects including Stein and Wright's Sunnyside, Queens (see fig. 27). The other three—Otto Haesler's Rothenberg Houses (1930–32) in Kassel, Germany; Ernst May & Associates' Römerstadt development (1927–28) in Frankfurt am Main, Germany; and Oud's Kiefhoek housing (1928–30, fig. 41, also shown in Section 1)—were the only social housing examined at any length in the entire exhibition. The quite considerable European effort to eliminate nineteenth-century and even older substandard speculator-built dwellings, and to replace war-damaged stock, was thus marginalized. Façades, furthermore, were given greater attention than apartment interiors or floor plans; housing as art, as opposed to its solutions for social problems, took priority. The 1932 exhibition made it appear that the new architecture and its aesthetics were primarily in the service of wealthy villa owners and those responsible for erecting large public or entrepreneurial structures, and only secondarily concerned with social issues when, in fact, it was the other way around.

But this was in keeping with the ideological bent of the Museum of Modern Art (MOMA). It was founded in 1929 by an exceptionally wealthy group of postimpressionist-art collectors including Abby Aldrich Rockefeller (treasurer), wife of John D., Jr.; Anson Conger Goodyear (president), a lumber merchant and banker; Francis Welch Crowninshield, a publisher, art editor, and artist; Professor Paul J. Sachs of Harvard, director of its Fogg Art Museum, formerly partner in the Goldman and Sachs banking house; and Mrs. Winthrop Murray Crane, wife of the president of Crane & Company paper mills and general manager and director of the

41. (top and bottom) J.J.P. Oud, Kiefhoek (1928–30), Rotterdam, The Netherlands. *Courtesy Royal Institute of British Architects*

Otis Elevator Company. Its stated purpose was to foster the appreciation and study of modern art, which it did by renouncing the customary museum practice of adding piece by piece to permanent installations in favor of temporary exhibitions, although from the start it built up substantial holdings to feed them, supplemented by loans from around the world. Its presentations were ordinarily retrospectives showing both the antecedents of a subject and its contemporary relevance—that is, historical sources said to have stimulated modern imaginations, like the influence of African traditional sculpture on Giacometti, for instance, and then, in turn, how Giacometti's sculptures influenced other kinds of work, like depictions of the human form in advertising or movie posters.

This required careful scholarly research, which was inclined to assign historical significance to art objects, not in and of themselves, but insofar as they informed present-day production (including use value) and insofar as they were made important retroactively by current taste. In American architecture, for example, because Henry Hobson Richardson could be shown to have influenced Louis Sullivan, who influenced Wright, who influenced the international style, Richardson was deemed a protomodernist; but since Richard Morris Hunt was not similarly influential, he had no contemporary standing. Therefore, Richardson, but not Hunt, was shown at MOMA. The present thus gave meaning to the past and its meaning was that it eventually became the present or, more accurately, a carefully selected *part* of the past became part of the present. And the part of all art, historical or modern, most thoroughly ignored at MOMA was its political, social, or any other kind of content beyond its formal properties.

Once this ideological position was established, it was sent out to do missionary work. Before the end of the 1930s, MOMA's film program offered free admission to members, distribution to scores of educational institutions nationwide, a research library, an information service, and a course on history and technique at Columbia University. For other arts, MOMA organized lending and noncirculating libraries, published a bimonthly bulletin and numerous exhibition catalogues, and set up committees for the advancement of modern art in thirty cities. Half of its eighty-five exhibitions by 1939 went on tour to over three hundred institutions. The 1935 Van Gogh show alone was seen by 142,000 people in New York and by 800,000 others from Toronto to San Francisco.

By 1939 MOMA was a national institution and *the* national center of modern art, setting a new standard for aggressive pursuit of museum policy.

By then, Lillie P. Bliss, one of the founders, had donated 235 works and treasurer Abby Aldrich Rockefeller an additional 181. (MOMA was already paying off as a tax deduction, having raised the value of its founders', lenders', and donors' holdings by vigorous promotion that successfully transformed "modern artists" into "old masters.") With its rapidly growing inventory, larger quarters were needed; these were provided in 1939, on Rockefeller-owned 53rd Street land originally intended for Rockefeller Center, by architects Philip L. Goodwin and Edward Durell Stone in what the AIA *Guide to New York City* calls "*a catechism* of the International Style: . . . an austere street front of marble veneer, tile, both opaque and transparent glass" that the WPA *Guide to New York City* said was a "rich but simple setting for the display of art."

There were two noteworthy features to this design. One was only partially executed. MOMA was originally conceived as part of a complex including the luxury Rockefeller Apartments, two buildings fronting on 55th Street and on 54th where its court was to double as the museum's sculpture garden. This was all constructed (fig. 42), the housing first, in 1936, to designs by Wallace K. Harrison, then working for the Rockefeller Center planning team, and by his partner, French-born André Fouilhoux, whose continuous contact with his native country explains why the apartments so closely resemble modern dwellings for the Paris affluent. The part of the complex not constructed was a midblock esplanade to run past the museum, linking the apartments' 55th Street front to 48th Street well within Rockefeller Center. Mayor Fiorello La Guardia's plan to develop the midblocks of 51st and 52nd Streets as a municipal art center akin to latter day Lincoln Center— dovetailed nicely with Rockefeller's, whose privately owned thoroughfare (which was in fact built, but only from 48th to 51st Street, and named Rockefeller Plaza) would have been the spine of a public ensemble defined by his apartments and museum to the north and his Center on the south.

Rockefeller's first idea for the esplanade route had been a 51st-to-55th-Street boulevard of luxury shops to compete with those on Fifth Avenue (which he did not own). Neither scenario materialized because the "Club 21" restaurant, directly in its path,

42. Philip L. Goodwin and Edward Durell Stone, Museum of Modern Art (1939), New York, showing Wallace K. Harrison and André Fouilhoux, Rockefeller Apartments (1936) with rounded bays in the background. *Courtesy The Museum of Modern Art, New York*

refused to relocate. But the fact remains that MOMA's original purpose was to be the cultural component of what in 1939 the *WPA Guide* called the "largest [commercial construction] ever undertaken by private enterprise," a playground for very rich New Yorkers living on 54th and 55th Streets, and a kind of private preemption of public culture (had the La Guardia art center materialized). All this represented one sort of social appropriation: of modern art and architecture for investment purposes and to legitimize commercial activity. And since the style of Goodwin and Stone's building was unfamiliar and undoubtedly off-putting to the general public at the time, it was also the latest indication of rarefied upper-class connoisseurship.

The other noteworthy feature of MOMA's new edifice was the marble, a material historically associated with luxury and building splendor but *not* associated with the new architecture (Mies's 1929 Barcelona Exhibition pavilion is one exception), *especially* not with the social housing that in Europe comprised the bulk of that work. This represented a second sort of social appropriation: of an architecture for the masses by those who ruled the masses. More than any other building in the United States in 1940 (Mies had not yet built at IIT, nor Gropius at Harvard), MOMA typified the international style of which it was also the most culturally visible example, as well as the first revelation of the elite's new public façade.

HEGEMONIC MODERNISM,

1940–1970s

WITHIN A YEAR or two Mies's initial building at IIT, for Minerals and Metal Research, was under way, the first of twenty-one low-rise structures (fig. 43) he designed for the campus before retiring in 1958, not all of which were built. The majority were clad in welded-steel frames painted black and sheets of glass, spanning up to twenty-four feet without interruption in the case of the 1952–53 Commons Building. The steel-and-glass system moved off campus to his twenty-six-story twin apartment towers (1949–52) known as 860–880 North Lake Shore Drive, Chicago, as did his reinforced concrete column-and-girder system, used sparingly at IIT, to the twenty-one-story Promontory Apartments (1948–49) on the South Drive. These buildings and his other work soon received enormous publicity, notably from the New York-based *Architectural Forum*, which helped bring him to national attention with a 1952 feature story. Even before the great fanfare accompanying his 1954–58 Seagram Building (fig. 44) in New York (in association with Philip Johnson, an up-and-coming acolyte) and his numerous but slight variations on the same themes nationwide—mostly towers, many in his adopted city—Mies was "sufficiently influential," according to Carl Condict, a devotee of Chicago architecture, "to produce a steady stream of derivatives."

That was a huge understatement. Mies imitators were countless, foremost among them Skidmore, Owings and Merrill (SOM) beginning with Lever House (1952) in New York. Here the frame was pulled behind glass-curtain walls (fig. 45)—non-load-bearing external walls hung between or over columns and not carried by the floors they pass—so as to be invisible from the street, a device Mies adopted at Seagram and with greater assurance after that, for instance at the 1959–64 Federal Center in Chicago. Although

43. Ludwig Mies van der Rohe's model of master plan (1940) for Illinois Institute of Technology (Chicago) campus. *Photo by Williams & Meyer Company. Courtesy The Art Institute, Chicago, Duckett Collection*

he had proposed the idea himself as early as 1919, the skyscraper curtain wall first appeared, but only on two façades, at the 1947–53 United Nations headquarters designed by an international team of architects including Corbusier, although Wallace K. Harrison did most of the actual work. After 1952 the glass wall, curtained or not, was everywhere, and as buildings in the 1960s and 1970s regularly reached sixty and seventy stories, spreading beyond the traditional limits of city blocks, they not only gobbled up perfectly serviceable tenements, workplaces, streets, even neighborhoods, but they also became the most visible constructions in the nation. It was difficult to ignore SOM's John Hancock Center (1965–70) in Chicago when it reached a hundred stories and 1,170 feet only to be surpassed by its Sears Tower (1970–74), also in Chicago, at 110 stories and 1,454 feet slightly higher than Minoru Yamasaki's World Trade Center (1962–77) in New York. In its twin 110 story towers, however, the Trade Center contained 10 million square feet, seven times the area of the Empire State Building, and consumed more energy than the city of Poughkeepsie (fig. 46).

From the early 1950s into the 1970s, Miesian derivatives in high-rise and low spread across the nation. Not since Richardson's

44. Ludwig Mies van der Rohe (with Philip Johnson), Seagram Building (1954–58), New York.
Photo by Ezra Stoller, courtesy Joseph E. Seagram and Sons, Inc.

45. Skidmore, Owings and Merrill, Lever House (1952), New York. Photo © by Ezra Stoller.
Courtesy Esto Photographics

work was seized upon by hordes of imitators in the 1880s and
1890s had a U.S. architect been so influential. And the why of it
is no mystery. Mies's buildings were deceptively simple and very
easy to copy: measure the distances separating horizontals and
verticals, vary their proportions, get a good structural engineer,

46. Minoru Yamasaki and Associates (with Emery Roth and Sons), World Trade Center (1962–77), New York. A New York Times *photograph*

add a touch or two of one's own (change the color, curve a surface, chamfer the corners, stick in diagonals) and the result was part of the canon. SOM was better at this than most. Its four-story Manufacturer's Hanover Trust Building (1953–54) in New York, for example, is a crisp jewel of metal, glass, and light (fig. 47), possibly

47. Skidmore, Owings and Merrill, Manufacturers Hanover Trust Company Building (1953–54), New York. *Photo by Robert Twombly*

the most visually arresting bank (at the time of its construction) since Louis Sullivan's in the 1900s and 1910s; its hundreds of structures since adhere to a high standard of handsomeness, dignity, and technological excellence. But, in general, quality went down as quantity went up. Drab, characterless behemoths stood shoulder to shoulder in every U.S. city, including some that never before had skylines. Mies was not responsible for the mediocrity of what was built in his name, but he *was* responsible for launching an architecture of aloof anonymity. And those ubiquitous glass boxes—rectilinear, sharp-edged, flat-roofed, artistically banal, and repetitive, repetitive, repetitive—were the preferred symbol of corporate America for close to thirty years.

The point is not that everything was curtain-walled, or even mostly glass, but that so much of it was featureless, regardless of material, following MOMA's 1939 lead. Featurelessness was not unintentional, however, and it took on increasingly ominous overtones as the years passed. Three examples: Harrison, Abramovitz and Harris's 1973–74 extension of Rockefeller Center for the Celanese, Exxon, and McGraw-Hill corporations—dubbed the "XYZ" buildings because they are almost identical and lined up in a row, each on its own block (fig. 48)—shot uninterrupted narrow granite columns alternating with uninterrupted window tiers of the same width over sixty stories straight up from sunken plazas. At One United Nations Plaza (1969–76), Roche, Dinkaloo & Associates covered upward of seventy stories with an unvarying glass and aluminum grid the *AIA Guide* said resembled "folded graph paper" (fig. 49). And in Boston, I. M. Pei wrapped the 1969–77 John Hancock Tower's sixty-five stories in four-by-eleven-foot mirrored glass panels (which kept falling out [fig. 50], much to the irritation of passers-by).

These buildings and many others like them reveal corporate priorities from the 1950s into the 1970s. First there is unreadability: these façades give little indication of where the floors are, where supports are located, if interior spaces differ from each other, in short, of anything going on inside, human or otherwise. They are also antisocial: mirrored glass, said to conserve energy and to be "contextual" by reproducing surroundings, acts as a self-

48. Harrison, Abramovitz, and Harris, the Celanese, Exxon, and McGraw-Hill ("XYZ") buildings (1973–74), New York. *Photo by Robert Twombly*

49. Roche, Dinkaloo & Associates, One United Nations Plaza (1969–76), New York. *Photo by Robert Twombly*

50. I. M. Pei, John Hancock Building (1969–77), Boston. *Photo by Robert Twombly*

protective barrier: one can see out but not in. Such glass at the
gigantic scale of both UN Plaza and the Hancock Tower is, furthermore, a deliberate snubbing of older, low-rise masonry neighbors that in Boston include Richardson's Trinity Church and
McKim, Mead & White's Public Library, and in New York the
Fred F. French Company's Tudor City, all distinguished land-
marks. And the huge scale of high-rise buildings like these is a
statement of corporate arrogance: established at XYZ by row after
vertical row of hundreds of feet of granite, so overpowering, so
cold, brutal, and intimidating, particularly when multiplied by
three, that years after construction pedestrians still cross Sixth
Avenue to avoid them.

The appeal of Miesian anonymity had to do with the changing
ways big business had been perceived since the 1930s and the
ways in which it perceived the social and political climate. Inves-
tigations into World War I profiteering, coupled with the general
understanding that corporate and financial machinations had
brought on the Depression, changed the image of the business
leader from rugged individualist culture hero to rapacious culture
villain. For corporate heads and managers, a new public façade

was in order and it was demonstrated, first of all, in personal styles. For post-World War II generations of the industrial and commercial elite—some of whom were now grand- and great-grandchildren of founding patriarchs—entrepreneurial swash-buckling was out. As time sanitized wealth, Ivy League educations, association with the arts, and charitable donations indicated cul-tivation, refinement, and good taste. A low but socially responsible profile was in. As individuals in the postwar world, the rich were seldom seen and even less heard except as society's benefactors.

On the level of personal architecture this meant unloading gaudy ancestral mansions like hundred-room Newport "cottages" or lux-urious "Gold Coast" town houses—if the latter, usually at great profit, given their prime locations—by Richard Morris Hunt and other "society" architects, in order to purchase completely invisible triplex apartments or secluded country retreats, like those designed in the late 1960s and early 1970s by a new generation of visible, socially connected architects. Robert A. M. Stern, for example, and "The Five"—Michael Graves, Peter Eisenman, Charles Gwathmey, John Hedjuk, and Richard Meier—all in their late thirties or early forties, worked for the well-to-do (fig. 51) in cool, neo-Miesian, neo-Corbusian vocabularies early in their careers when they were mostly doing houses.

Nineteen-fifties and -sixties corporate architecture also reflected these considerations, plus one other: that big business had been diversifying and consolidating simultaneously, becoming identified less with single products than with ranges of servicing, manufac-turing, marketing, and investing divisions. Ownership had become anonymous, dissociated from individual names. Against a back-ground of the changing structure of large-scale enterprise and the negativity with which it had been perceived after the stock market crash of 1929, postwar corporate ownership, now building on a large scale for the first time in fifteen years, appropriated what it understood to be salient characteristics of 1920s and 1930s Eu-ropean and U.S. modernism: cool competence, understatement, restraint, rationality, minimal disclosure, an international outlook, and, most important, technocratic efficiency spurning historical association. When applied to the skyscraper, the international style was made to be aloofly impersonal, almost blank, hardly revelatory, completely reversing the pre-Depression New York style (compare fig. 52 with fig. 53) but elaborating Chicago School mannerisms.

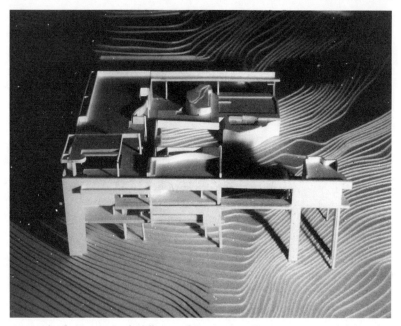

51. Michael Graves, Rockefeller residence project (1969), Pocantico Hills, New York. *Courtesy Michael Graves, Architect*

The new façades were tabulae rasae, on which to rewrite the past by promising a more benign future, one akin to that proposed by "social engineering" intellectuals like economist Walter Rostow and sociologist Daniel Bell, who argued that corporate domination guaranteed security and prosperity for all.

But with all this, of course, the international style was altered beyond recognition. New corporate façades bore no relation to structure or specific function: they simply covered everything over. They were neither symmetrical nor asymmetrical. They were not so much visually striking—in the Chicago School manner (or that of Gropius, Lescaze, or Hood), making something of the relationship between solids and voids—as they were minimally patterned, often without direction or depth, like Scotch plaid but not as varied or lively. They eliminated ribbon windows, overhanging roofs, and cantilevers—anything giving façades texture or movement—and by the 1970s emphasized mass as often as volume. But they were not designed for *human* masses except, of course, for masses of clerical employees. If European architects of the 1920s had given serious thought to housing thousands of residents in what they believed were congenial, healthy, and uplifting buildings, postwar corporate architects gave minimal thought beyond productivity considerations to housing hundreds of thousands of workers behind façades that, if they implied anything on the subject, deemed employees to be interchangeable drones performing interchangeable tasks in interchangeable spaces. But, of course, these buildings were less about workers' than about corporate interests.

And those interests reached an apogee of architectural expression with the movement called "total design" in which everything inside a building was subject, according to *Life* magazine in 1966, to "the new world of centralized esthetic planning." In their Eero Saarinen-designed 1961 headquarters in New York, Columbia Broadcasting System (CBS) officials "watched over every detail, from . . . the shape of ashtrays [to] the style of numbers on elevator buttons," from "the species of 899 plants used painstakingly throughout the building" to their "varieties and hues . . . in each color area." At SOM's American Republic Insurance Company head-

52. Midtown Manhattan in 1975.

53. Lower Manhattan circa 1941. *Photo by Ewing Galloway*

quarters (*c.* 1963) in Des Moines, "every clerical desk in the building is of the same design so that . . . the people themselves . . .
become the decoration."

At CBS, *Life* reported, "furniture and its precise placement has
been carefully preselected and it may not be moved. Office 'accessories' such as ashtrays, pencil holders and in and out boxes
are standardized and may not be replaced by personal versions.
Except for these accessories, desks and table tops should be left

clean, unadorned by personal superfluities. Mementos and gadgets, even family pictures, are frowned upon. Potted plants are provided by the company and watered weekly by 'monitoring teams'. Employes may not grow their own plants, nor touch or water company plants. Walls must remain bare except for art works selected, framed and hung by the company. These may not be moved. No personal art may be hung without specific approval of the director of design." At American Republic, in addition, desk-tops were to be cleaned and left bare overnight, each chair and covered typewriter placed on a precisely prescribed spot until morning (fig. 54).

Why this "centralized esthetic planning" down to the minutest detail? Because, according to Louis Dorfman, director of design at CBS, who was pointing to a group of secretaries while being interviewed, "you can't let *them* lead. You'd get chaos. Just pick ten people around here and go into their homes and that's what you'd see. Chaos. Look at the so-called glories of individualism . . . at the old CBS building. *Idiot* scrawls on the walls, second-rate artistic choices. That's individualism for you." "Nobody works as individuals," agreed Watson Powell, Jr., of American Republic. "This is a team effort."

54. Skidmore, Owings and Merrill, American Republic Insurance Company Building (c. 1963), Des Moines, Iowa. *A* Life *photograph*

"Left to their own devices," *Time* summed up this kind of corporate thinking, "the individual employee is apt to run rampant, flaunting his bad taste, creating what [design directors] refer to with clenched teeth as a 'rabbit warren' or a 'Kewpie doll atmosphere'. . . . They view the average worker as an esthetic child needing discipline from more sophisticated superiors to route his actions along approved channels." Or, as one American Republic official put it: "People are permitted to work in the most beautiful, most dignified, quietest working conditions in America" for the purpose of achieving "imposed discipline." A prime justification for "total design," *Time* concluded, "is said to be efficiency," "efficiency tied in with a new corporate interest—art. Herein lies the key to the whole concept of corporate control."

But corporate control was never total. Workers grumbled, and in small ways refused to comply with the "dozens of rules and regulations" prescribing their relations with their work environments. When they complained, at CBS, they were rebuked, or found their minor adjustments undone by what they referred to as "gremlins" or "the Gestapo," or even by President Frank Stanton during his "frequent inspection patrols." Board Chairman William S. Paley, on the other hand, ignored total design, loading up his office with thick draperies, personal mementos, and French antiques. The individualism so abhorrent in workers could not, of course, be denied to Paley, whose own version of a "Kewpie doll atmosphere" stood in direct violation of company policy.

Paley's statement of personal power, over and beyond that of CBS, represented in microcosm the gradual abandonment of cool detachment in favor of an architectural arrogance seen in the blank massiveness of his own building's façade, in the XYZ, United Nations Plaza, and John Hancock behemoths, and in other corporate edifices. In point of fact, the fine line between Miesian understatement and assertions of raw power was increasingly crossed during the 1960s. But Paley also anticipated something else.

Just as he broke the design rules by which all others were bound, so did corporations in the 1970s begin to reject two decades of received architectural wisdom. Belatedly understanding that public hostility had waned, that the political climate was again friendly, that muscle flexing would go unchallenged, they launched a search for more appropriate imagery. The generalized hostility of the 1930s and early 1940s had actually diminished considerably during

55. Emery Roth and Sons, Colgate-Palmolive (1955), International Telephone and Telegraph (1960), and Manufacturers Hanover Trust (1960) buildings, New York. *Photo by Robert Twombly*

56. William Pereira & Associates, Transamerica Building (1972), San Francisco.
Courtesy Transamerica Corporation

the 1950s, in effect rendering superfluous the corporate stampede toward Mies's style. But then, business had purposefully selected that sleek, ahistorical image, perhaps without considering or perhaps knowingly embracing its built-in contradiction: that when replicated in building upon building, side by side, on street after city street, anonymity brought with it loss of company identity. For the ultimate in corporate conformity, see New York's Park Avenue from 47th to 52nd Streets where stand SOM's Union

57. Philip Johnson (with John Burgee), American Telephone and Telegraph
Building (1978), New York. *Courtesy American Telephone and Telegraph Company Photo Center*

Carbide Building (1960) and the Banker's Trust (1963), Colgate-
Palmolive (1955), International Telephone and Telegraph (1960),
and Manufacturer's Hanover Trust (1960) buildings by Emery
Roth & Sons, especially the nearly indistinguishable last three (fig.
55), as well as most of the west side of Sixth Avenue from roughly
44th to 57th Streets.

Compromising corporate identity may have been a small price
to pay (or a cowardly way, or a shrewd ploy) for recapturing public

approval, but in the 1970s it no longer sufficed. Possibly taking a
cue from 1960s "lifestyle" politics, corporations began to realize
how much they had denied themselves by clinging so long to
conservative Miesian formulas. William S. Paley's personal nose-
thumbing at the rules gradually became collective and institutional.
Conspicuous early departures from the glass box and the featureless façade were eye-catchers like William Pereira & Associates'
Transamerica Building (1972) in San Francisco, an elongated pyramid with twenty-story shoulder-like projections on two sides, rising straight from the sidewalk to a needle-like point some 853 feet
up (fig. 56); Hugh Stubbins & Associates' 1977 Citicorp Center
in New York, a 900-foot tower with the top 130 feet sliced off at
a forty-five-degree angle; and Philip Johnson and John Burgee's
1978 American Telephone and Telegraph Company Building (fig.
57), also in New York, with a three-quarter round cutout at the
apex of a faux gable looking like a Chippendale breakfront. Aside
from these heavy-handed gimmicks, none of the three exteriors
(or interiors) departed from modernist canon. But they signaled
that visual differentiation was again a corporate priority. So the
Transamerica Building became the company logo and Citicorp
Center a much-publicized New York icon, while AT&T is sometimes said to have inaugurated in skyscraper design what quickly
came to be called "postmodernism."

MODERNISM'S FAILURE:
PUBLIC HOUSING,

1 9 4 9 – 1 9 7 0 S

IF "MODERN" HAD CAPTURED U.S. architecture in the 1950s primarily through high-profile commercial skyscrapers, it rapidly permeated all design genres—in the form of flat-roofed minimalisms (fig. 58) with lots of glass held together by metal or concrete—as far down the ladder of social hierarchy as invisible architects worked, that is, to the point at which developers took over. There, in the vernacular, middle-class housing—no longer of interest to visible architects in the postwar era—represented a compromise between traditional and modern. In ranch and other kinds of houses, "new" consisted of lower, longer, simpler silhouettes, carports or built-in garages, picture windows in front and glass doors opening on patios in back, perhaps "split" levels with play (later family) rooms downstairs, dens above for dads, and, for moms, up-to-date kitchens off the dining "ells" of "open" plans. "Old" included gabled or slightly pitched roofs vaguely recalling bungalows or the Georgian, remnants of trim around doors and windows, wood construction, little-used walks leading to still-formal front entrances, occasional brick chimneys, and similarity with neighbors.

Modernism also filtered down to working-class dwellings, especially to public housing for a new generation of "very poor"—now including welfare clients and increasing numbers of people of color—during postwar "urban renewal" campaigns. By the late 1940s, the housing crisis had become too acute to ignore. Its causes are fairly obvious. During the fifteen years of depression and war from 1930 to 1945, annual nonfarm permanent dwelling unit starts (as determined by building permits issued) had fallen to less than one-third the average of the eight years beginning in 1922. Di-

58. Beach house, Deal, New Jersey. *Photo by Robert Twombly*

minished purchasing power throughout the Depression, followed
by unavailability of materials during the war, forced landlords and
owners to defer maintenance and repairs. Immediate postwar oc-
cupancy rates close to 99 percent meant that apartments were not
to be had. Two or three generations crammed into aging, deteriorating buildings—still expensive to improve or replace during
a postwar inflationary surge—was rapidly becoming the norm for
middle-income but especially for poor people.

Response to the crisis took the form of federal subsidy for the
private sector. According to Title I of the 1949 Housing Act,
Washington would pay municipalities up to two-thirds the price
of purchasing and clearing land, in completely or partially rundown neighborhoods, that could then be sold at favorable rates to
developers whose taxes would presumably cover the remaining
start-up costs. Immediately after passage construction soared, from
998,000 new residential units in 1949 to 1,352,000 the next year,
not dropping below a million annually, a level never reached before
1950, until 1957. Publicly owned housing also surged, from 18,000

new units in 1948 to 71,000 in 1951, before gradually tailing off. But demand far exceeded supply. Federal officials estimated in 1950 that over 5.7 million city-dwellers lived in "substandard" units and in the nation as a whole one-eighth of the entire population. Housing experts contended, however, that reality in the first instance was closer to 10 million and in the second, a quarter of the nation, or 36 million people. Thus the 1954 Housing Act, which introduced the term "urban renewal"—the 1949 legislation had spoken of "urban development"—was designed to accelerate construction by making private investment even more rewarding. Ten percent of federal grants could now be used for nonresidential purposes, later raised to 35 percent, with only 25 percent of housing in a district needing to be "substandard" to qualify for renewal funds.

Despite these and other incentives, the low-income housing crisis remained just that. Building and maintaining apartments for poor people at affordable rents was simply not sufficiently remunerative to attract large-scale private investment. Thus "urban renewal" was often referred to sarcastically as "Negro removal" because it frequently meant replacing poor minorities in conveniently located neighborhoods with middle- and upper-income tenants. Between 1949 and 1968, for example, less than one-third of the "deteriorating" low-income housing units that were razed were replaced in the same or nearby locations, and over half of that one-third were luxury apartments. Gross figures—ignoring who actually lived or was put where—were also disheartening. From the construction of the nation's first public housing in 1934 until 1970, federal, state, and local governments erected a total of 893,000 living units (143,000 of which were for the elderly), which is exactly the same number built by the private sector in the single year 1924 and which, in 1970, housed less than 2 percent of the U.S. metropolitan-area population.

Though never put up in adequate numbers, low-income housing nevertheless achieved a certain architectural distinctiveness in style, scale, and location. As the years passed after 1949, state and municipal authorities increasingly preferred to build massive high-rise clusters of factory-, warehouse-, and prison-like appearance in remote or rundown districts of no interest to developers. The Public Works Administration had imposed a four-story height limit that, like the New York Housing Authority's First Houses (1935) and Harlem River Houses (1937), fit comfortably in their older, walk-up neighborhoods; prewar public housing, in other words, was intended to blend into its built environment. Postwar construction, by contrast, was made to stand out and, as a corollary, to stigmatize its residents.

One intellectual underpinning of postwar public housing in the United States was yet another architectural appropriation of a European model, this time Corbusier's "towers in a park." Beginning in 1922 and repeatedly thereafter during a long career ending with his death in 1965, Corbusier advocated huge, freestanding towers, set in green space, removed from vehicular traffic, as the solution to urban housing shortages. Although his Voisin Plan of 1925 would have razed much of central Paris, a proposal many thought somewhat short-sighted, he believed that light-filled, well-ventilated, roomy flats with broad terraces, huge vistas, and access to garden-like surroundings would improve spiritual and physical well-being for all classes of people. His social objectives cannot be faulted even if his architectural means were highly dubious. But in the United States it was his means—"towers in a park"—rather than his objective that was seized upon. Corbusier was one of the two or three most influential architects of the twentieth century, but it was this idea—no fault of his that others corrupted it—with which he made his greatest impact.

Corbusier had envisioned gleaming glass and concrete skyscrapers carefully placed in expansive gardens and parks; urban renewal, with the commonest of brick and small scattered windows, built high-rise barracks jammed cheek by jowl on empty concrete wastes in the middle of existing, inconveniently located slums. Corbusier had envisioned his towers as new kinds of city centers; urban renewal built new kinds of urban backwaters. The buildings were "modern" in that they were flat-roofed, sharp-edged, unornamented, and basically monochromatic, but it was modern architecture of the most debilitating sort. In tandem with 1956 federal legislation creating the Interstate Highway System, urban-renewal housing accomplished its social objective quite well: the physical banishment of the poor and minorities to out-of-sight, out-of-mind areas of town.

In South Side Chicago, for example, the Dan Ryan Expressway, twelve lanes wide plus a rapid-transit median strip, is lined for two miles by the 1964 Robert Taylor Homes (fig. 59), a fifteen-block-

59. Chicago Housing Authority, Robert Taylor Homes (1964). *Courtesy Chicago Historical Society*

long, one-block-deep string of twenty-eight identical sixteen-story brick structures housing some 27,000 African-Americans. Horizontal roadway and vertical buildings combine to create a terrifying demiworld of over-, through-, and underpasses that no one dares traverse by foot at night, a virtually impenetrable barrier walling off vast "white ethnic" neighborhoods to the west from vast African-American slums to the east. In 1980, 90 percent of Robert Taylor's 4,300 families were headed by women living below the federal poverty line. Median family income was $3,800. The project contained less than one half of 1 percent of Chicago's population, which was subjected to 9 percent of the city's rapes, 10 percent of its aggravated assaults, and 11 percent of its homicides. Unemployment in the Robert Taylor Homes was 47 percent. Chicago's way of dealing with the social consequences of poverty and racism was apparently to hide them behind walls called public housing.

But Chicago policy was hardly singular. One of the few public-housing projects by a visible architect, in this case Minoru Ya-masaki, was the award-winning Pruitt-Igoe Houses (1952–55) in St. Louis, thirty-three eleven-story orange-brick buildings containing 2,800 units and 12,000 people. Pruitt-Igoe was award-winning in part because of its modernist design featuring south-facing, window-lined "galleries" on every floor intended as "outdoor" areas for socializing, play, eating, even sleeping. Yama-saki's professional peers also praised his cost-effective elevators stopping at only the first, fourth, seventh, and tenth floors—so that 70 percent of the tenants had to walk up or down a flight after getting off—as well as his laundry and storage rooms con-venient to galleries on the upper three elevator levels.

By 1966 the laundry and storage rooms were locked and sealed, and no one ate or slept on the galleries where few youngsters played without parental supervision. The elevators proved entirely inappropriate for unaccompanied small children, who, in the nor-mal course of events, were escorted up or down dimly lit stairwells to reach them; in another increasingly normal course of events, elevators were jammed at floors on which they did not open in order to mug passengers. Tenants objected to exposed pipes and conduits (some architects considered this stylistically avant-garde), to unpainted public areas, dark narrow hallways, and small rooms (residents were supposed to spend leisure time on the galleries), and felt belittled by strict rules governing pets, paint colors, over-night guests, and use of washing machines. When the buildings opened, 52 percent of resident families were self-supporting; by 1973, ten years after the city began moving in welfare clients at the same time cutting budgets for security and maintenance, 85 percent received public assistance. When the buildings opened, they were racially integrated even though erected in an African-American slum; by 1973, they were almost entirely black.

Because of restrictive rules, constricted space, pressure to adopt approved lifestyles, and the elevators, some units were never rented and the vacancy rate always exceeded the 5 percent national average for federally subsidized projects. By 1972, only 340 of the 2,800 units were occupied. Virtually abandoned by the city, the complex became such a sinkhole of pestilence for those with no choice but to remain, constantly attacking it and constantly subject to criminal attack, that the municipality dynamited three buildings in 1972 and razed the remainder two years later. International television coverage enabled the world to see the worst failure in U.S. public-housing history, including the enormous gap between what low- and no-income people needed and what government officials and prominent architects thought they should have.

Standing out almost alone from the many Pruitt-Igoe failures is Taino Towers, whose design by the invisible firm of Silverman & Cika was approved by the Department of Housing and Urban Development (HUD) in 1971 but not completely realized until 1983. Delay came from federal mismanagement, from those opposed to participation during planning stages by neighborhood advocacy groups, and from strenuous objections to its unusual (for low-income housing) features. Located in East Harlem, New York City, its 656 units, including some with six bedrooms and two and a half baths, are contained in four thirty-five-story towers of concrete and glass "so well detailed," one architecture critic remarked, "they could have been done by Skidmore, Owings, and Merrill." Apartments have parquet floors, spacious closets and terraces, floor-to-ceiling windows, central air-conditioning, large rooms, and, in the public areas, there is a swimming pool, a gymnasium, greenhouse, a closed-circuit television system with production capacity, an auditorium, a thousand-seat outdoor amphitheater, laundry rooms next to rooftop playgrounds, a day-care and a medical center, and commercial space in which residents might work or open small businesses. Rental priority went first to those displaced by construction (over 250 families returned), then to other neighborhood people.

Taino Towers represented the largest single outlay HUD ever made for public housing, more than $67 million over the life of the mortgage—or less than the cost of one Vietnam War helicopter—plus rent subsidy for 40 percent of the apartments in which families pay no more than 25 percent of their incomes. "We could have built smaller units with fewer facilities and gotten more apartments for the price," commented a community-based Taino administrator in 1974, "but we were trying to make a change in people's lives, not just create another future slum." The strategy at Taino Towers, making it so different from other public housing, was to link decent living space to job training and provision (retail outlets, flower and vegetable growing, television and theatrical production), to make it easier for those with jobs to keep them (day-care and medical service), and to encourage tenant interaction and collective pride in place. In 1980, with two buildings fully and a third partially occupied, there were over six thousand applicants for the remaining three-hundred-odd apartments. Taino Towers was working. But "my understanding is this is a unique experiment," a HUD official explained that year; there were "no plans to duplicate it elsewhere." So began and ended an urban-renewal venture in well-designed, carefully thought out, architectural modernism that in middle-class circumstances would have been praiseworthy, but that *The New York Times* referred to perversely as "low-income luxury."

NONCOMMITTAL
ECLECTICISM, 1970s–1990s

THERE WAS PLENTY of luxury, to be sure, elsewhere in U.S. architecture, but very little stylistic agreement. Beginning in the 1960s, a number of new design currents grouped practitioners in so many stylistic camps that by the 1990s—as in the 1890s—an updated eclecticism was again in full swing. For all intents and purposes, modernism itself was reduced to a single current among many. The more notable developments, all of which left residues for later architects to draw upon, included the "new formalism" or neo-neoclassicism of the 1960s—strictly symmetrical structures with columns and arches, overhanging flat roofs, ornament in the form of metal grilles or patterned masonry, and smooth, shiny, usually expensive materials—mostly reserved for institutional edifices: embassies, libraries, museums, cultural centers, and the occasional corporate headquarters. Minoru Yamasaki, Philip Johnson (fig. 60), and Edward Durell Stone were prominent in this vein, and prominent buildings included New York's Lincoln Center (1962–68) by several architects, the Amon Carter Museum of Art (1961) in Fort Worth and the Sheldon Memorial Art Gallery (1963) in Lincoln, Nebraska, both by Johnson. "Neo-expressionism"— nonrectilinear, curving, sculpted work, often with sweeping reinforced-concrete shells, distantly based on 1920s designs by German Expressionists Hans Poelzig, Erich Mendelsohn, and others—was best executed by Eero Saarinen at Dulles International Terminal (1960) in Chantilly, Virginia, at Yale University's 1956–58 Ingalls Hockey Rink (fig. 61) in New Haven, and at the Trans World Airlines Terminal (1962) at John F. Kennedy International Airport, New York.

"Brutalism" of the 1960s and early 1970s requires a lengthier

60. Philip Johnson, Pavilion (1965) at Philip Johnson residence, New Canaan, Connecticut. *Photo by Robert Twombly*

61. Eero Saarinen, Ingalls Hockey Rink (1956–58), New Haven, Connecticut. *Photo by Robert Twombly*

treatment because of its disturbing social implications, as well as its aesthetic departures, and because of what Louis I. Kahn—the most recent U.S. architectural master—did with it. Brutalism derived from the work of Peter and Alison Smithson in England and from late Corbusier, particularly his Unité d'Habitation (1945–52) in Marseilles and his Couvent de la Tourette (1954–56) near Lyons. Characterized by heavy, massive concrete forms left rough, exposed utility conduits, boxy or slab projections and insets creating dark shadows and deep penetrations of a building's mass, it was most often used for government, educational, and occasionally religious edifices. Paul Rudolph is closely associated with brutalism in the United States. His Art and Architecture Building (1958–64) at Yale, designed during his tenure as chair of the Department of Architecture, illustrates the style's social meaning.

As realized in New Haven, brutalism (fig. 62) is an architecture of rejection and impenetrability. Entries are tucked under downward-bearing cantilevers or at the rear of slots cut into the building. Enter at your peril, it seems to say. There is plenty of glass but it is beyond reach or visible access from the street. We can see you but you cannot get at us, is the message. Its chunky blocklike forms in rough concrete and its jagged profile turreted against the sky suggest a bunker. Inside, its staggered levels and complicated spaces flow into each other vertically and horizontally, making visual surveillance easy but circulation confusing, as if the medieval street system of Venice, arranged self-protectively to confound invaders, had been compressed into a single building. Physical and aural privacy are in short supply but not skin abrasions from too intimate contact with the walls. The Art and Architecture Building proved its worthiness in 1969: when out of anger and frustration students set it afire, they caused considerable damage but could not burn it down. The only casualty was Rudolph, who had already resigned. (On the other hand, when his 1965 Christian Science Student Center in Urbana, Illinois, outlived its usefulness in the late 1980s and the Church was unable to sell it after exploring every alternative for its use, it was demolished.) Perhaps it was only coincidence that student upheavals of the 1960s touched off a wave of similar campus constructions raised up on berms, platforms, or stilts, encasing everything in concrete with tiny windows and few, easily sealed entrances. Among the many examples are the science centers at the City College of New York and the State

62. Paul Rudolph, Art and Architecture Building (1958–64), New Haven, Connecticut. *From John Jacobus,* Twentieth Century Architecture: The Middle Years, 1940–1965

63. Kallman, McKinnell and Knowles, City Hall (1963–68), Boston. *Photo by Robert Twombly*

University of New York, Stony Brook, and the Elvehjem Museum–
Humanities Building complex at the University of Wisconsin,
Madison.

At the Boston City Hall (1963–68), Kallman, McKinnell and
Knowles applied brutalism to government structures (fig. 63). Sitting at the foot of a vast, empty, windswept plaza, it is raised on
concrete girders and pylons of varying height up to the equivalence
of about five stories. Entrance through and under them is belittling
enough, but arrival in the huge atrium-lobby with inadequate indication of where next to proceed is especially disorienting. Its
exterior, however, is far from ambiguous. High above the plaza,
massive concrete projections in different shapes indicate city
council and school committee chambers, the mayor's office, and
the like. Higher still, as if in the servants' mansarded attic of a
nineteenth-century town house, small protruding fins designate
dozens of identical clerical cells. And why not cells at Boston City
Hall, based closely as it is on Corbusier's convent near Lyons? But
in Boston they suggest nothing about community, nothing about
the public-service aspects of republican government. Rather, with
its clearly stated hierarchy of power and its formidable presence,
City Hall stands as a fortress against assault, a 1960s icon of the
state under siege.

Marcel Breuer's 1966 Whitney Museum of American Art in
New York embellished this imagery with drawbridge and moat,
perhaps implying that the cultural heritage could at any moment
be barricaded from the public, and when the city itself replaced
its 1909 Beaux Arts police headquarters in 1973 with a Gruzen &
Partners late-brutalist design, it sent out a similar signal. Indeed,
precinct houses for police and fire departments across the
nation—not to mention urban high schools, courthouses, and
National Guard armories (fig. 64)—were commonly made crowd-
repelling. Compared to turn-of-the-century government architecture, its successors sixty and seventy years later asserted power
more blatantly. They were equally monumental, even more self-
defensive, but not at all historical. The Roman Empire no longer
offered a secure visual harbor for the ship of state. When the "new
radicalism," the civil rights and anti-Vietnam War movements, and
other protest activities dissipated in the 1970s, U.S. cities were
left with numerous architectural testimonies to the most recent
period of social unrest that should stand them in good stead for
the next one.

64. Charles S. Kawecki for the New York State General Services Administration, 42nd Division Armory (1971), New York National Guard Building, New York. *Photo by Robert Twombly*

Brutalism had a certain influence on Louis Kahn. His First Unitarian Church and School (1959–69) in Rochester, New York, and his Indian Institute of Management (1962–74) in Ahmedabad show its traces. But they, along with the Phillips Exeter Academy Library (1965–72) in Exeter, New Hampshire, his government structures (1962–83) in Dhaka, Bangladesh, and others of his buildings are among this century's finest. The Jonas Salk Institute for Biological Studies (1959–65) in La Jolla, California, may be his very best. Its three components—research laboratories, housing, and community center—form an approximate U-shape, the latter two sitting on bluffs overlooking the Pacific. Farther back, two parallel blocks of laboratories terminate at a pool from which issues an extremely thin channel of water bisecting the plaza between them (fig. 65). Visually, the channel extends to infinity, linking laboratories to sea, whose murmurs roll on gentle breezes back along the plaza, which is hushed, tranquil in the sun. Trees rustle in the wind, shading outdoor seating, and form a border for the entire complex except where completed by the ocean. Fire, earth, air, and water—the sun, the landscape, the breezes, and the sea —unite here in serenity. All this to encourage the collective labor of a human community for the common good. At its best, this is what architectural design can sustain and represent.

No one whose practicing career reached maturity after Kahn's death in 1974 has yet equaled his genius, but in each of the remaining late-twentieth-century architectural currents there is at least one standout. "Neo-" or "late modernism" refers to metal, glass, and concrete architecture evolving directly from pre- and post-World War II precedents. Smooth-surfaced and taut-skinned, but with more color and variety of form than was possible before the 1970s, it is well represented by Cesar Pelli, Gwathmey Siegel, Hardy Holzman Pfeiffer, and the Chicago office of Skidmore, Owings, and Merrill, especially in their corporate and institutional work. Richard Meier sets an unusually high standard of excellence for his late-modernist colleagues, if not for the entire profession, with his exquisite detailing, his daring forms often executed in stunningly pure white materials, his subtle balance of delicacy and strength, and his success accommodating user needs. Among his best efforts are the Atheneum (1975–79) in New Harmony, Indiana; the 1980–83 High Museum of Art (fig. 66) in Atlanta; the administrative offices and production center (1991) for Canal Plus, a Paris television station; and his Santa Monica, California, J. Paul

65. Louis I. Kahn, Jonas Salk Institute for Biological Studies (1959–65), La Jolla, California. *Photo by John Lobell*

66. Richard Meier, High Museum of Art (1980–83), Atlanta, Georgia. *Photo by E. Alan McGee. Courtesy The High Museum of Art Public Relations Office*

Getty Center, an enormous complex of interconnected structures designed and erected during the 1990s.

"Postmodernism" is sometimes used as an umbrella term for architecture in general during the 1980s and early 1990s, referring to the undeniably widespread historical eclecticism of the time. But it is more accurate to apply the term to individual buildings and architects rather than to the profession as a whole. Among the key postmodernists are the late Charles Moore, Robert Venturi, Stanley Tigerman, Robert A. M. Stern, Michael Graves, Helmut Jahn, and Philip Johnson, who, throughout his career, has moved from style to style, taking up the latest fashion. Visually, postmodernism means a great deal: the return of polychrome, ornament, and traditional design elements (like gables, "Palladian" windows, conical roofs, classical orders, pediments, and elaborate moldings), and it means experiments: with trapezoidal and other improbable shapes, giant color fields including stripes, tilted towers, complicated profiles, protrusions, recessions, and extrusions, a kind of madcap mixing and unmatching of almost everything in frenzied ostentation. In some ways this has been liberating for the profession, particularly younger architects, who benefited from its anything-goes attitude devoid of what had become modernist rigidities. The high-rise work of Kohn Pederson Fox demonstrates the artistic possibilities and creative form-making that can result from thoughtful application of this new design freedom (fig. 67).

But socially, postmodernism means nothing new, because, despite claims to the contrary, it took as its own the prevailing social relations of architecture, certainly with regard to the fundamental component of those buildings with which it made its greatest mark: worker space in corporate skyscrapers was in no substantial way reconceived. On the other hand, the social meaning of postmodernism is clear: in relation to urban amenity and to society at large, corporations will do as they please. Since skyscrapers of the 1980s tended to be bulkier than their modernist predecessors, and closely packed together in the nation's downtowns (see Johnson's "Crescent," c. 1985, luxury housing and upscale shops in Dallas, and his 1980s schemes for the Times Square, New York, redevelopment), although not yet taller—nothing has surpassed Sears Tower despite several proposals to do so—what it pleased corporations to do was colonize ever greater amounts of air, land, sunlight, and energy, cause unprecedented congestion, and place unparalleled strains on urban infrastructures, all the while further dismantling older, perfectly viable neighborhoods. For all their stylistic showmanship, postmodern skyscraper owners have been profoundly antisocial in their treatment of cities and employees, and profoundly reactionary in their commitment to an increasingly inegalitarian social order. Although their buildings looked new and dazzling, they were, in their fundaments, testaments to private plundering of the public realm. Postmodernism, in other words, achieved new heights of arrogance. It was the perfect architecture for the Ronald Reagan years.

It had its determined apologists, to be sure, who argued that modernism had destroyed urban milieus, made itself incomprehensible to the public by shunning historical association, was overly monumental and artistically sterile (Venturi's reply to Mies's famous minimalist dictum "less is more" was "less is a bore"), and was launched either by insensitive egomaniacs (Mies, Corbusier,

67. Kohn Pederson Fox, Bank of the Southwest project (1982), Houston. *Photo by Jack Horner. Courtesy Kohn Pederson Fox*

Wright) or by socialist zealots as a plot to construct a proletarian paradise (presumably, 1920s European social-housing designers). To remedy these failings, postmodernists advocated "contextuality" ("fitting" buildings "in" their surroundings, too often, alas, by mimicry), the reintroduction of premodern design features and of lively color and bold form, and refraining from claiming too much for their art—for example, the early modernist contention á la Ruskin that good architecture could enrich private life and contribute to social harmony. (Some argued the opposite, in fact: that good architecture awaited the good society, a way, perhaps, of relieving designers of social accountability.)

In design terms, some of these contentions were on the mark, and the new work did on occasion visually enliven daily life, as well as retrieve familiar design elements—like sash windows and roof gables—people seemed to prefer. When it was sensitively contextual, it bound together rather than fragmented its surroundings, but, in fact, most of the new work disrupted built "context" even more than modernism had. Politically, postmodernist claims were self-serving. The "socialist plot" accusation, for example, fit all too well with the national retreat from housing the poor. It also ignored the obvious lack of commonality between Mies's willingness to work with Nazis as director of the Bauhaus and Philip Johnson's 1934 founding of a "Gray Shirt" organization supporting Huey Long, on the one hand, and commitment by outspoken socialists and social democrats to universal housing reform, on the other. In short, postmodernism might better be regarded as artistic self-indulgence—as elite art for elite art's sake—than as a serious critique either of the history or of the social meaning of design.

As the 1980s ended, postmodernism began to fade, proving itself a short-lived fad (which is not to say its mannerisms disappeared, especially not from the vernacular, where they remained firmly entrenched), but some of its adherents, along with others never involved, had already drifted into "deconstructivism" or "deconstruction." Said to be based at least in part on the impenetrable texts of French philosopher Jacques Derrida, "decon" maintains that if "truth" and "reality" exist, they are virtually impossible to discover and thus reside, if anywhere, in the slippery realms of subjectivity. Contemporary life, furthermore, is cruel, dangerous, and without real meaning except as an arena for pointing that out. The wisdom of the ages can safely be ignored because it has obviously failed to enlighten humanity or alleviate its condition. There are no absolutes; all is relative. For architecture this means that rules exist to be broken. Why should a staircase not rise to a blank wall or a door not open directly on a fat column, obstructing forward movement? Life is like that: full of the unexpected, of unanticipated obstacles, of impediments to progress, of failed plans. Public pronouncements by Philip Johnson during his latest transformation endorsed the architectures of Frank Gehry, Eric Owen Moss, French emigré Bernard Tschumi (dean of architecture at Columbia University), and others—including decon's most prominent practitioners, who are European, and Americans who dabble in it occasionally—which share certain characteristics: angularity, seemingly disconnected parts, knifelike edges and slashlike openings, flying struts and other ephemera, walls out of plane and floors off level, joints that appear not to mesh and cantilevers threatening to collapse, that is, potpourris of jarring, incompatible elements, some adapted from 1920s Soviet constructivism but used in the 1990s to foster an architecture of optical illusion suggesting impermanence, uncertainty, apprehensiveness, risk, even danger.

Peter Eisenman shuns the deconstructivist label but his work partakes of its aura and constitutes a benchmark against which it might be measured. The title of a 1994 essay about him, "Repulsion Is the Attraction," hints at his design ambiguity but does not capture the complexity of his intentions. His Greater Columbus (Ohio) Convention Center (1991) is an interpretation in agitated forms and striking colors of the commercial and railroad architecture formerly on the site and, with a number of highways, still surrounding it. What appear to be ten elongated, slightly bent, abutting structures with roofs and façades canted at varying angles, is actually a 218,000-square-foot divisible hall with attached support services. Inside, what seem to be skewed, disjointed, crazily juxtaposed spaces become upon inspection organized "streets" and "squares"—as in a village—bringing a sense of order and manageability to an enormous volume. And also inside, what looks at first glance to be a purposefully disorienting, structurally unsturdy, indeed collapsing area (fig. 68) proves to be a playful stairwell lobby for socializing and unplanned encounters. By basing his architectural language in Columbus on a memory of the site and on tangible needs of the present, Eisenman found ways to transform a gigantic rupture with the past into a continuation of it, in

68. Peter Eisenman, Greater Columbus (Ohio) Convention Center (1991). *Photo by D. G. Olshavsky/*
ARTOG

forms conditioned by contemporary sensibilities. If, in the hands
of some, deconstruction means a license for glib avant-gardism,
for Eisenman it reflects a contemporary angst that might nevertheless be harnessed to architectural advantage.

By the mid-1990s even deconstruction was waning. At Frank
Gehry's prototypically decon American Center (1992) in Paris, for
example, a collage of jagged forms resembling paper cutouts jostled
each other for viewer attention, but for his 1994 Disney Corporation ice-skating rink (fig. 69) in Anaheim, California, he abandoned that nervous, stitched-together fragmentation in favor of a
lump spreading across the site like a squashed mushroom: the
triumph of the couch potato over the neurotic. So much for stylistic
continuity. But Gehry's turnabout was not atypical. Just as new
formalism, neoexpressionism, brutalism, and other currents since

69. Frank Gehry & Associates, Mighty Ducks Skating Rink (1994), Anaheim, California. *Photo by Joshua M. White. Courtesy Frank Gehry & Associates*

the 1960s faded from fashion but bequeathed residues to a bulging grab bag of forms and possibilities, so did postmodernism and deconstruction further intensify the "anything goes" climate of stylistic noncommitment evident in both the profession at large and in the work of individuals. By the 1990s most elite architects were adapting ideas from history and from each other while daily inventing startling forms that invisible architects and developers borrowed willy-nilly. There were some—Richard Meier, Kohn Pederson Fox, Peter Eisenman, and others not mentioned: Booth Hansen in Chicago; Shepley, Bulfinch, Richardson & Abbott in Boston, and Davis, Brody in New York among them—whose work was stylistically consistent, indicating ongoing examinations of firmly held convictions. But in general, the plethora of razzmatazz, mix-and-unmatch assertions in every conceivable manner had the effect of canceling itself out, creating of itself a collectively homogeneous eclectic mainstream wherein every building proclaimed an individuality that very few had.

Nothing was further removed from this frenzied homogeneity than what could still be called "organic" architecture. Evolving from Frank Lloyd Wright's late work at his rural Wisconsin and Arizona residences, this earth- and nature-oriented design was further developed in very disparate ways in the houses of Bruce Goff and Herbert Greene (both lived and worked in Norman, Oklahoma), in Paolo Soleri's futuristic "Arcosanti" village (begun

c. 1956) near Scottsdale, Arizona, not very successfully by Wright's former apprentices and by Taliesin Associated Architects, his successor firm (he died in 1959), and even in urban areas by those latching onto the unanticipated revival of interest in Wright that soared during the 1980s. The luminary in this genre is Fay Jones, whose chapels, residences, and other small buildings out of Fayetteville, Arkansas, are among this century's most beautiful. His handsome dwellings are noticeably Wrightian, but his chapels— especially the wood, fieldstone, metal, and glass memorial (1988) for Mildred B. Cooper tucked into a dense grove of trees near Bella Vista, Arkansas (fig. 70)—may be the most sensitive, elegant, and original interpretations of the Gothic in this nation's history. But they are more than that, for Jones has transformed it into eloquent expressions of his own time and place and of the sites on which his buildings stand. They are Gothic in the same way Henry Hobson Richardson's work was Romanesque, which is to say, they have evolved far beyond their initial inspiration to become unique, personal statements. Although organic architecture has not been taken up by prestigious design schools, the reexamination of Wright, together with Jones's 1990 award of the AIA's gold medal for excellence, suggest that even the profession's elite recognizes this out-of-the-mainstream work as a vital font of good design.

70. Fay Jones, Mildred B. Cooper Memorial Chapel (1988), Bella Vista, Arkansas. *Photo by Timothy Hursley*

AT CENTURY'S END

AS LONG AS MODERNISM was hegemonic, interest in Wright was low, sustained through the 1960s and 1970s by the occasional scholarly appraisal and gallery show. But during the 1980s sober consideration of a great architect was pushed to the distant reaches of a marketing blitz led by a self-duplicating assault of publications: the 1992–93 *Books in Print: Titles* with eight entries for Corbusier, nine for Palladio, and eleven for Mies van der Rohe, has a staggering fifty-five for Wright—Abraham Lincoln had a very impressive seventy-three but Franklin Roosevelt a mere twenty-six —and together with *Authors* and *Subjects* offered readers about a hundred Wright books (not counting dozens of others recently unavailable). With the books came endless conferences and symposia, innumerable shows and traveling exhibitions, walking tours, television programs, an opera, and plain old commercial savvy: by 1990 it was possible to drink from a "Frank Lloyd Wright" coffee mug, hang his likeness on the wall or wear it on a T-shirt, listen to his speeches on record and to songs about him on cassette, purchase "Frank Lloyd Wright" neckties, notepaper, dinnerware, cutlery, candlesticks, vases, rugs, lamps, furniture, and lots more, even mobile homes, and pay several hundred dollars to spend a weekend at one of his former estates.

That no other U.S. architect has come even close to being so lionized, or so commercialized, is illuminating for what it recalls about Wright himself, for what it suggests about the uses to which he was put thirty or more years after his death, and for what together they reveal about the state of his profession at the close of the twentieth century. Wright was one of the great, possibly *the* greatest, architectural self-promoter of all time, and he did it

113

with panache. Possessing a deep, mellifluous voice, a flair for the theatrical, a taste for the brash, a ready wit and a sharp tongue, he was much in demand as a public speaker and in the 1950s as a television guest of Mike Wallace, Hugh Downs, and Jinx Falkenberg and Tex McCrary. He gave innumerable interviews and wrote hundreds of newspaper and magazine articles and close to twenty books. His comments were biting, trenchant, and often outrageous, combining an uncompromising certainty, no matter the subject, with scandalous asides and barbed witticisms.

He was politically outspoken—a staunch opponent of Senator Joseph McCarthy and the House Subcommittee on Un-American Activities—and on design matters he was an unforgiving critic of the glib and the trendy, which for him included the work of Mies van der Rohe, "Little Philip" Johnson, Corbusier, and, with very few exceptions, every other architect since the Renaissance. *His* work, of course, was never glib or trendy, and he exploited it brilliantly, especially during the 1950s when he announced his most startling proposals at carefully choreographed press conferences complete with striking visual props. Wright was rarely out of the limelight, in fact, during his last decade or more, having made himself a living legend well before he died. So in one sense the 1980s fuss about him simply picked up, after a brief hiatus, where he had left off.

By then, many visible architects, if not exactly emulating Wright, were assiduously following him to the limelight, though not with his flamboyance, since his all-American brand of folksy immediacy was no longer de rigueur; publicity departments and media consultants now supplied the preferred image of coolly sophisticated world citizen. But in point of fact, Wright was to his profession as Polaris is to the firmament: the first to shine in the new architectural star system. Television miniseries, newsweekly feature stories, regular columns in metropolitan dailies, glossy magazines peeking into "homes" of the rich and famous, bookshop departments of expensive monographs, stores devoted exclusively to architectural bric-a-brac, toney galleries and chic auction houses—all promoted the profession and its "stars." Wright could not have anticipated the extent to which architecture would be commodified but he, or rather others in his name, garnered its benefits. Even posthumously, he remained the brightest star of those promoted: in the 1990s there were no songs about Philip Johnson and no I. M. Pei T-shirts.

Visible architects were willing collaborators in the commodifi-
cation process, and with good reason. The mass marketing of things
architectural, as opposed to architecture itself, became a handsome
source of supplemental income in the 1980s when office over-
building of the previous decade brought new high-rise construction
to a virtual halt, when soaring interest rates meant that few middle-
class people could afford to purchase a residence and fewer still
to hire an architect. Except for years of depression and war, the
decade was one of the most inactive for middle-class housing
production in this century, accelerating the postwar withdrawal of
visible practitioners from the field. Concentrating on corporate,
institutional, and commercial work when they could get it—many
firms reduced staff significantly during the 1980s—elite profes-
sionals also began in a major way to market self-promoting "archifacts." Aside from omnipresent Rizzoli publications (for the
coffee table next to *Architectural Digest*) there was furniture by
Richard Meier and Robert Venturi for Knoll International and
jewelry by Meier, Venturi, Stanley Tigerman, Cesar Pelli, Michael
Graves, and others for Cleto Munari of Vincenza, Italy. There
were tea sets and birdhouses by these and others equally visible,
glowing fish lamps by Frank Gehry, and a cookie tin by Graves
(which could be carted off in his Bloomingdale's shopping bag)
replicating his 1980 Portland (Oregon) Building. Even those who
had not built anything ("paper architects," they were called) sold
their drawings and published their books. (This is not a contradiction: during the 1980s a number of architects whose designs
had not yet, and in some cases never, left the printed page and
the drawing board became international stars; perhaps for the first
time, worldwide visibility could readily precede rather than follow,
and sometimes generate, actual commissions.)
    The archifact served as the mass-marketing agent of postmod-
ernism. It stimulated interest among, and extracted money from,
those for whom owning architecture could only mean owning
something about it. It was class-unconscious: whereas Gehry's fish
lamps sold for thousands, Graves's cookie tin was only twenty
dollars. Perhaps, like elaborate cornices on turn-of-the-century
tenements, the lower end of postmodern marketing was meant to
assure "everyperson" that architects still cared. (It is somewhat
peculiar to the profession that, the further its practitioners remove
themselves from actual contact with and design for ordinary people, the more insistently they proclaim that their work responds

to life as lived.) And just as postmodern eclecticism extended modernism's homogenization of historical and regional design distinctions, so did the archifact render all stars and styles equally desirable and important. Philosophical difference and political or social orientation mattered less than sales potential and prestige by association, which meant that Frank Lloyd Wright finally became acceptable to the Museum of Modern Art.

He had never been entirely ignored there, of course, if only because he was too important (and noisily insistent upon it). But MOMA was never comfortable with Wright. He was not an urban sophisticate; he lived in the country, regularly attacking cities, especially New York. His work was difficult to categorize; it was, but then again was not, "modern," at least according to MOMA's definition. And most important, even before the Museum was established in 1929, Wright had openly opposed the new European architecture it espoused. It included him in its 1932 "Modern Architecture—International Exhibition" nevertheless, but "only from courtesy," wrote Philip Johnson, one of the organizers, "and in recognition of his past contribution." That was true. Three of Wright's five depicted buildings had been designed more than twenty years earlier and were the oldest on display; they had, continued Johnson, "nothing to say today to the International Group." Remarks like this hardly endeared MOMA to Wright.

The Museum gave him a kind of one-man show in 1940. "Frank Lloyd Wright: American Architect" was a retrospective to that date. His late-1930s creative explosion—including Fallingwater, the Johnson Wax Administration Building, Taliesin West, and continuing explorations with his new Usonian House—was difficult to ignore, especially in light of the enforced slowdown of architectural progressivism in Europe at the time, and it clearly put the lie to the 1932 implication that he was a has-been. It was a "kind of a one-man show" because he shared the spotlight with filmmaker D. W. Griffith under the heading "Two Great Americans," a peculiar pairing that did not improve Wright's relations with the Museum.

From 1938 to 1959 MOMA presented single Wright buildings on five occasions, and five other times included something of his in large, thematic shows. Not until three years after he died did he receive undivided attention: a 1962 exhibition of some three hundred drawings. There was a small display of new Fallingwater photographs the next year, and in 1967 he appeared in a show on urban renewal. All this, which is actually not much, should not obscure the fact that the national guardian of modernism never held a full-fledged retrospective for the nation's foremost, home-grown, modern architect. Mies van der Rohe, by contrast, had two: in 1947, on the cusp of his becoming the dominant force in U.S. design, and a more extensive one in 1986, seventeen years after he died, to commemorate his birth centennial. (MOMA also houses the Mies archives.) He had been ideologically acceptable there, of course, and publicly much kinder to it than Wright, who, despite his undeniable importance in twentieth-century architec-ture, was consigned, in New York, to its periphery.

If enough is at stake, however, ideology can and will be com-promised. But it was still a shock to the art world in 1975 when MOMA mounted a major exhibition on the architecture of the École des Beaux-Arts, not previously understood to have been a bastion of things modern. Either the third word in MOMA's name had been redefined or the museum was signaling the drift toward historicism even before it was deemed cutting edge enough to be dubbed *post*modern. But equally surprising in retrospect as in-corporating nineteenth-century academic conservatism into the twentieth-century avant-garde canon was that it took the Museum almost another twenty years to get around to Wright.

The 1994 "Frank Lloyd Wright: Architect" exhibition was the most lavish and comprehensive tribute to his work ever staged. With 190 buildings depicted on two floors, it far surpassed the scale of Mies's 1986 centennial, but it broke no new scholarly or interpretive ground and was thus, it might be said, a triumph of packaging. Its timing was also significant. The craze for Wright, the architectural star system, and the mass marketing of archifacts were already well established when the show was being planned, making it a safe, if not inevitable, undertaking, considering also that no other architect, dead or alive, was "bigger" than Wright at the time. Then, too, the decline of postmodernism and the short-lived appeal of deconstruction—which had originated in Eu-rope, anyway—left those in need of guidance adrift on a rudderless architectural ship. "The Wright exhibition . . . now offers an all-American alternative," Joseph Rykwert wrote in an insightful re-view. "A whiff of architectural xenophobia is in the air again."

These perceptive observations require qualification. Architectural xenophobia, a real possibility given the political climate at home and abroad, will be mitigated by the further international-ization of firms and forms that had accelerated after World War II. Many visible practitioners now maintain offices in more than one country and take commissions around the world, in the process influencing architects everywhere. Signature and even generic buildings in Hong Kong, Berlin, or New York are increasingly less dependent on local cultural traditions and personal design idio-syncracies than on globally shared mannerisms and the interna-tionalization of capital. Like calls for trade embargos, movement toward an "America first" architecture will bump up against what might be called "the new world order." And if there is to be an "all-American alternative" to postmodernism or deconstruction, it will not be Wright's. Sporadic, localized revivals of his work pre-ceded deconstruction's arrival, were actually part of postmodern-ism's historicizing, and do not seem to be increasing, although the MOMA show could stimulate a new mimetic flurry. But any move toward Wright will be superficial, another fad, another eclectic strand, if only because, unlike Mies's work, his was too personal, subtle, and complex—too difficult for most practitioners to digest in all its fullness—to be the basis of a fundamental reorientation of national design.

The most suggestive observation in Rykwert's review is this: "The presence of Philip Johnson at all the Wright events—at the parties, in symposia, on television—is significant," he wrote, re-ferring to the elaborate hoopla accompanying the show. "Johnson remains a one-man litmus-paper of architectural fashion," and his "patronage guarantees that a new fashion in American architecture has begun. In his day he was a 'modernist', but he also produced some of the more unhappy examples of post-modernism." Then "he launched the Deconstruction exhibition and manifesto [a 1988 MOMA show and catalogue assembled under his direction]. Now that . . . Johnson has adopted Wright, we are obviously in for a national change of style."

Throughout his long career—he was born in 1906—Johnson has demonstrated an uncanny ability to spot new trends almost before they begin. But he is not an originator. More an architec-tural symptom than a cause, a bellwether than a soothsayer, if he now designs according to Wright, as he did for Chicago in 1986 according to the Chicago School (with special reference to John

Root), it will likely be for one or two buildings until the next fad comes along. If a shift in fashion is what Rykwert meant by "change of style," he will be proved right. But if Johnson's newfound interest means something more essential, that the nation's elite is reexamining Wright for more profound reasons, then Rykwert will again be correct, because if anyone knows what is in the wind it is Johnson. If change is coming, however, he will not initiate it despite intimate ties to those in power. Johnson has cried wolf too often, has gone through too many stylistic transformations to be trusted with such responsibility. And he is too old. But if social conditions are right, other architects will be available.

A fundamental change in national style—on the order of the postwar shift to modernism—necessarily presupposes not more eclecticisms but their elimination, and that presupposes a change in demand by wielders of power, which, if Rykwert is correct about Johnson, is in the offing. The shift away from modernism toward a menu of fairly well-defined design currents in the 1960s and 1970s, then to a groaning smorgasbord of possibilities in the 1980s and 1990s, was the consequence of a protracted architectural identity crisis among the individuals, particularly in their corporate and institutional capacities, who direct the nation's political, economic, and cultural agendas. That identity crisis involved serial reappraisals of the social climate that, in the end, brought about today's stylistic *non*commitment. Commitment to a new style, or styles, will likely depend on whether the unraveling of civil society in the United States becomes threatening enough to convince the elite to pursue architectural reformulation. If that happens, not "neo-Wright" but another round of neoclassicism or even a "new" brutalism will open the next century. It remains to wait and see.

SELECTED BIBLIOGRAPHY

This brief listing includes books that are pioneering (either in choice of subject matter or in method), that are comprehensive, or that are important contemporary documents.

The most reliable overview of twentieth-century architecture in the United States is contained in the appropriate chapters of Leland M. Roth, *A Concise History of United States Architecture*, rev. ed. (New York, 1996). William H. Jordy's volumes 4 and 5 of the "American Architects and Their Buildings" series are brilliant and indispensable: *Progressive and Academic Ideals at the Turn of the Twentieth Century* (New York, 1972) and *The Impact of European Modernism in the Mid-Twentieth Century* (New York, 1972). Marcus Whiffen, *American Architecture Since 1780: A Guide to the Styles*, rev. ed. (Cambridge, Mass., 1992), parts 4–6, is an excellent introduction to particular mannerisms.

There are innumerable studies of the Chicago and prairie schools. Carl W. Condict, *The Chicago School of Architecture: A History of Commercial and Public Buildings in the Chicago Area, 1875–1925* (Chicago, 1964) is comprehensive, as is H. Allen Brooks, *The Prairie School: Frank Lloyd Wright and His Midwest Contemporaries* (Toronto 1972), which is also reflective and stimulating.

For interpretations of high-rise buildings that are in varying degrees challenging, see Paul Goldberger, *The Skyscraper* (New York, 1981); Ada Louise Huxtable, *The Tall Building Artistically Reconsidered: The Search for a Skyscraper Style* (New York, 1984); Thomas A. P. van Leeuwen, *The Skyward Trend of Thought: Five Essays on the Metaphysics of the American Skyscraper* (The Hague, 1986); and Piera Scuri, *Late-Twentieth-Century Skyscrapers* (New York, 1990).

The literature on housing, though vast, is spotty. The best overview is Gwendolyn Wright, *Building the Dream: A Social History of Housing in America* (New York, 1981), parts 4 and 5 especially. New York is better served than other cities by Richard Plunz, *A History of Housing in New York City* (New York, 1990), chapters 4–10.

For local design "culture," see: Reyner Banham, *Los Angeles: The Architecture of Four Ecologies* (New York, 1971); Douglass Shand Tucci, *Built in Boston: City & Suburb* (Boston, 1978); M. Christine Boyer, *Manhattan Manners: Architecture and Style, 1850–1900* (New York, 1985); and Donald Bluestone, *Constructing Chicago* (New York, 1991).

Studies of modernism in general with material on the United States include: Sheldon Cheney, *The New World Architecture* (New York, 1930); Bruno Zevi, *Towards an Organic Architecture* (London, 1950); Nikolaus Pevsner, *Pioneers of Modern Design: From William Morris to Walter Gropius*, rev. ed. (New York, 1960), and *The Sources of Modern Architecture and Design* (London and New York, 1968); Dennis Sharp, *Modern Architecture and Expressionism* (New York, 1966); Charles Jencks, *Modern Movements in Architecture* (New York, 1973); Vincent Scully, *Modern Architecture: The Architecture of Democracy*, rev. ed. (New York, 1974); Kenneth Frampton, *Modern Architecture: A Critical History* (London, 1980, 1985); Bill Riseboro, *Modern Architecture and Design: An Alternative History* (Cambridge, Mass., 1983).

For modernism's arrival in the United States, see Henry-Russell Hitchcock and Philip Johnson, *The International Style: Architecture Since 1922* (New York, 1932), and Terence Riley, *The International Style: Exhibition 15 and the Museum of Modern Art* (New York, 1992).

Since the 1980s there has been a rash of monographs about individual practitioners. Studies of those treated at some length in this text that are also analytical include: George E. Thomas, Michael J. Lewis, and Jeffrey Cohen, *Frank Furness: Complete Works* (Princeton, 1991); Jeffrey Karl Ochsner, *H. H. Richardson: Complete Architectural Works* (Cambridge, Mass., 1982); Leland M. Roth, *McKim, Mead & White* (New York, 1983); Paul R. Baker, *Richard Morris Hunt* (Cambridge, Mass., 1980); Robert Twombly, *Louis Sullivan: His Life and Work* (New York, 1986), and *Frank*

Lloyd Wright: His Life and His Architecture (New York, 1979); Randell L. Makinson, *Greene & Greene*, 2 vols. (Salt Lake City, 1977–79); Thomas S. Hines, *Richard Neutra and the Search for Modern Architecture* (New York, 1982); Franz Schulze, *Mies van der Rohe: A Critical Biography* (Chicago, 1985) and *Philip Johnson: Life and Work* (New York, 1994); David Brownlee and David De Long, *Louis I. Kahn: In the Realm of Architecture* (New York, 1991).

Too many important U.S. designers now deceased—Walter Gropius, William Lescaze, Raymond Hood, Rudolph Schindler, Irving Gill, Clarence Stein, and Henry Wright, among them—await comprehensive treatment. On the other hand, the work of several important contemporaries—Robert Venturi, Michael Graves, Richard Meier, Fay Jones, among others—has been reproduced in handsome picture books.

For an alternative to U.S. professional practice, readers may wish to consult Herman Hertzberger, *Lessons for Students in Architecture* (Rotterdam, 1991).

INDEX